millie

antique & collectible Buttons

IDENTIFICATION & VALUES

Debra J. Wisniewski

COLLECTOR BOOKS

A Division of Schroeder Publishing Co., Inc.

The current values in this book should be used only as a guide. They are not intended to set prices, which vary from one section of the country to another. Auction prices as well as dealer prices vary greatly and are affected by condition as well as demand. Neither the Author nor the Publisher assumes responsibility for any losses that might be incurred as a result of consulting this guide.

Note: All buttons pictured throughout are shown close to actual size unless otherwise noted.

Searching for a Publisher?

We are always looking for knowledgeable people considered to be experts within their fields. If you feel that there is a real need for a book on your collectible subject and have a large comprehensive collection, contact Collector Books.

Cover design: Beth Summers
Book design: Sherry Kraus
Photography: Charley Lynch

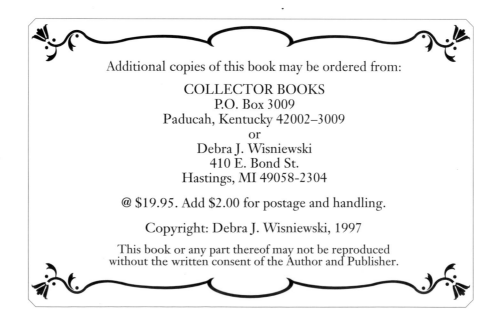

Contents

Acknowledgments

I would personally like to thank Doris Mohler, who back when I first started collecting was always willing to answer any questions I had, send button books and old issues of *Just Buttons* and *Nationals* to me, and always made me feel welcome to the button world. It really meant a lot to me at that time and still does. To the members of the Michigan Button Society, and my local club members of the West Michigan Buttoneers whose well wishes and enthusiasm have been greatly appreciated, I thank you!

Gary Embrey for his helpful information and pricing of the uniform and political buttons. Laurie Kilmer of White's Photography for the button mounting board. Irma Vajda, my friend and best button buddy, whose encouragement kept me going on a daily basis. To my editor, Lisa Stroup, whose kind words and reassurance made a wish come true. And to Gina Lage of Collector Books for her help in turning my manuscript into a book. Thank You!

I'd also like to thank my dad and mom, Gordon and Jane Barlow, whose endless love has given me the confidence to do this.

And last, but definitely not least, my husband, Tim, and son and daughter, Tyler and Ashley, who without complaint attend every button show, lug boxes of buttons from collections I've bought, put up with piles of unsorted buttons throughout the house, and when I slacked off on the housework working on the book, only complained a little. I love you, and yeah! it's all done!

Dedication

For Tim, Tyler, and Ashley
For Gordon and Jane Barlow

About the Author

Debra Wisniewski has been involved in her family's estate auctioneering business since 1970. She recently served three years as the president of The West Michigan Buttoneers and also served one term as secretary of the Michigan Button Society and is a member of the National Button Society. She continues to spread the joy of button collecting at schools, historical societies, and civic groups.

Introduction

"You collect what?"
"Buttons."
"Buttons?"
"Yes! Buttons."
"Political buttons."
"No! Clothing buttons."
"Oh, that's different..."
"Here, I have some pictures."
"Wow! These are buttons?"
"Yes."
"They were really on clothes?"
"Yes."
"Beautiful, unbelievable!"
"I've never met a button collector
before."
"Well, now you have!"

—DJW

Many button collectors, including myself, have had this very conversation. Be it your family pet, your love of gardening, or your appreciation of history and the fine arts, Egyptian, Oriental, and Indian culture, stories, sports, and mythology even a non-collector can relate to buttons in some form or fashion. That is their appeal to so many people. The purpose of this book is to give general information on the different materials and the broad range of subjects they covered. The prices are what I consider to be realistic, based on what I have paid and considerable discussion with other collectors. It must be said that it does not mean that the identical button has not been recently sold for more or less. I would like to express to the readers the importance of being a knowledgeable collector, spend a little extra money on books, join your local, state, and national societies. Share you knowledge with the new collector, and always remember that "Goofies" are just as interesting as eighteenth century.

HAPPY BUTTON HUNTING!

I Was Bitten by the Bug

It all started 10 years ago. Being from a family that is interested in antiques and collectibles it's no wonder my first buttons came from an estate auction. My husband, Tim, and I arrived to the auction late and there were only two tables of box lots left. Gee! What can I spend my money on? I don't think I've ever left an auction empty handed. Noticing four clamp-top jars of buttons in a box, I thought wouldn't that be fun to dig through? The auctioneer chants $10.00, $5.00, what'll bid? I'm an auctioneer's daughter and I had no fear of raising my hand to bid — I just couldn't decide *what* to bid! Up flies my hand, "$2.00," I say. "Anybody bid $3.00?…Sold to the young woman over there for $2.00!" When we got home the buttons went straight to the attic, sight unseen. I guess it wasn't the prize but the excitement of wanting to bid on something. Besides, they were just old buttons anyway. Six months later on a cold and damp day I sent Tim to the attic to retrieve the buttons. As I carefully dumped them on the table it was apparent to me that they were different from your normal buttons. What fun I had the rest of the afternoon sorting those little buttons.

Almost two years later, a mother/daughter auctioneering team advertised buttons to be sold at their auction house in Fowlerville, MI. The thought of driving 1½ hours for buttons was not received well by Tim, but I explained to him that I had called the auction house and the buttons belonged to a *real* button collector. Well, I never saw such pretty buttons. My heart was pounding. Thinking to myself, no one will notice them, I bet I'm the only person interested. I mean please, nobody really collects buttons, right? Each glass and wood frame had 42 glass buttons of the same color arranged in a special pattern. On the back of the frames was a ribbon that said "Michigan Button Society First Place." While I waited for the auction to start, several women were also checking them out. I was already coveting them and wanted to scream "Stop! Their mine!" Pink, green, blue, yellow, and white glass — which to buy and what to pay was racing through my mind. I said to Tim "What do I do? Should I keep bidding?" "Deb, we drove this far and waited this long, you might as well." I was the high bidder on two of the frames. I don't remember the exact dollar amount, but it was somewhere between $28.00 and $32.00 each. That was a lot of money for me, considering I didn't know anything about button prices then. I found out the woman who had owned the buttons was in the auction house. She had been collecting for about 30 years and had sold most of her collection to members in her club. "Club, what club?" I squealed. She handed me something that said Michigan Button Society on it. That was my introduction to the world of button clubs and shows. I soon learned there were a couple of collectors in a town north of me. I called a woman named Joyce and asked if she would be interested in starting a club with me. Joyce volunteered to hold the meetings at her house and we began meeting on Sunday afternoons.

A few months later, I had the chance to purchase some buttons that had been in storage for 18 years. The owner's first husband had been an antiques dealer. It had been many years since he passed away, and she was selling everything that had been in storage. The buttons were in bags and cigar boxes — enough to fill three large banana boxes. That was my first purchase of so many buttons at one time. I've recorded all my adventures in a button diary, but will save that for another time.

How You Can Get Started

Most collectors start out purchasing buttons at auctions, garage sales, flea markets, or antiques shows. Family members and friends are good sources too. I've always pushed new collectors to purchase button books, join your local and state clubs, and learn as much as you can before you start spending large amounts of money. I feel purchasing buttons from club members and button dealers is really the way to go. In general, antiques dealers do not know what makes a button collectible and tend to price their buttons much higher than a button dealer would. They are always willing to listen when you tell them they could probably ask a little more, but are very put off when you comment that their prices are way too high. Until you've gone to your first button show, it's hard to imagine the vast array of buttons available. With all that said and done, you can still occasionally get lucky at antique shows and shops.

Button Cleaning Tips

Glass

Most glass buttons have finishes that have been fired on and can be soaked in warm soapy water mixed with a little all-purpose cleaner. A light brushing with a soft toothbrush will get the heavy dirt off. Rinse and air dry on a towel. A word of caution, some paint finishes were not fired on. Unless you're sure what you have, do nothing or proceed with caution. If your glass is set in metal do not soak or allow water to enter the button. Instead, wipe with a damp cloth. Glass buttons that have rhinestone trim can be gently wiped with a cotton swab dipped in window cleaner. Just make sure you dab the swab on a paper towel first, so the excess does not run under the stones and loosen them. I also hold the button upside down while I wipe it clean, this seems to work well.

Brass

One-piece brass buttons have no rim or back and can be cleaned with most metal polishes. I keep a bag of worn-out cotton tube socks just for that purpose. Dried polish stuck in cracks can be scrubbed out with warm soapy water and a toothbrush.

Metal buttons with a rim or back should *never* be submerged in water. There is a cardboard disc inside all two- and three-piece brass buttons. If water gets to the disc, it will eventually ruin the button. It will either start rusting, or the disc will swell and separate the back and rim from the face of the button. I prefer two methods: 1) If the button is in very good condition and needs minor cleaning, a metal polishing cloth works well; 2) If the button is very tarnished, I use an electric erasing machine. You hold it like a pencil and the eraser tip spins around very fast. The tip is good for getting into cracks and crevices and is not as messy as metal polishes. Just brush out the eraser crumbs. You do have to be careful though, this will take off tints. Practicing on lesser quality buttons is a good idea to learn what you can and cannot do with this machine. It is important to buy a good quality machine because the cheaper models have problems with motors burning out, and *only* use the soft green eraser refills. This machine works very well on cleaning all metal shanks, too.

Enamels

Some collectors use metal polishes, but again I prefer to rub mine on a small square green eraser. It really cleans the metal on champlevé enamels. If the button is solid enamel, I wipe with a cloth and window cleaner.

Horn and Rubber

Neither types should be washed in water. I use Old English® oil or baby oil. Horn buttons can be attacked by bugs and mites. Some collectors put moth crystals in an envelope and slide behind the buttons in their display frame. Make sure you wipe off any excess oil so you don't ruin your mounting board.

Plastics

Plastics can be cleaned in warm soapy water. If they have other material trim or are set in metal, don't soak them in water, wipe with a damp cloth.

Wood or Wood Background

Old English® oil works well on all wood buttons. Be careful of any paint trim. Once or twice a year, I put Old English® on a cotton swab and apply it to my metal buttons that have the wood backgrounds.

Pearl

Most pearl buttons that are in good condition only need an occasional rubbing with baby oil.

Sometimes you come across ones that have a white powder-like appearance. This is caused by being in a container with other types of buttons for a long period of time. I've been told that steel wool and metal paste polish will take this off.

Final Tips on Cleaning

If you're a first timer, practice on broken or junk buttons. If there's more than one material, make sure you treat it appropriately. No matter what the face of the button is made of, if it is mounted in metal do not let water or any liquid seep into the button. If you're not sure what your button is made of or how to clean it, it is better to do nothing. With experience you will learn what to do.

I love my electric eraser, but you need to practice using it. I know what I can and cannot do with it. A button with patina is much more desirable than a button that is ruined from too much cleaning. Buttons should only be air dried, never put in an oven or clothes dryer. Don't forget to clean your metal shanks. If you see any rust or green scrape it off and rub with a green eraser.

Mounting and Storing

Whether you are a beginner or just have a few old buttons from grandma's button box, it is important to mount your buttons. The reason for this is that each type of button has it own chemical make-up. When the buttons have been enclosed in containers like jars, tins, or bags, they tend to destroy each other. Metal buttons start to rust, pearl buttons get a white powdery appearance, and celluloids and plastics warp and disintegrate. Dealers who sell button supplies have a variety of patterns already designed on board or mat cards. They also carry templates which allow you to draw the patterns on the board yourself.

Most collectors use plastic-coated telephone wire when mounting their buttons. Non-coated wire and pipe cleaners eventually rust and can cause damage. Lay your board on a double folded bath towel before punching the holes. I use a small wooden handled Phillips screwdriver that has been ground to a point. Thread the wire through the holes in the button or shank. Then put both ends of the wire in the hole on your board. If the button has a loop shank push the shank in the hole. Do not pull from the backside. You can break your glass buttons that way. Hold the front of the button against the board with one hand, and with the other, twist the wire in a coil against the board. I store my cards in hanging file folders. Just make sure your filing cabinet has drawers that are at least 12⅛" wide or the 9 x 12 cards that are required for competition will not fit. Vinyl folders and wood frames for displaying your buttons are also available from dealers.

Condition

There are many buttons to choose from and like other antiques and collectibles, condition is very important. Stay away from buttons that are scratched, chipped, rusting, or have worn paint or luster. The prices in this book are for buttons in very good to excellent condition.

Pricing

"You're crazy" and "Don't do it" are comments I heard from several collector friends when I announced my book would also include prices. Button prices are very erratic and I've resigned myself to the fact that no matter what prices I set, I will not please everyone. The last few years have seen a rise in new collectors, unknowledgeable dealers, and button auctions, drastically increasing the prices of buttons. Collectors buy for many reasons. A need to fill a competition tray or the attitude "I must own it at any price" play a large part in the outrageous prices paid for certain buttons. I truly believe this is only hurting our collecting field and may discourage future collectors. Do not assume the person selling the buttons knows more than you do. Study, shop around, and use your own best judgment as to their value. Most important, have fun!

Type of shanks found on most celluloid buttons.

Thread back.

Pad shank.

Backs of old metal buttons.

*Backmarks L-R: Eingetragen (registered),
T.W.&W (Trelon, Weldon & Weil) Breveté (patented),
AP&Cie (Albert Parent and Company),
Geschutzt (protected).*

David & Ettie West
East Jewett, New York, 1925

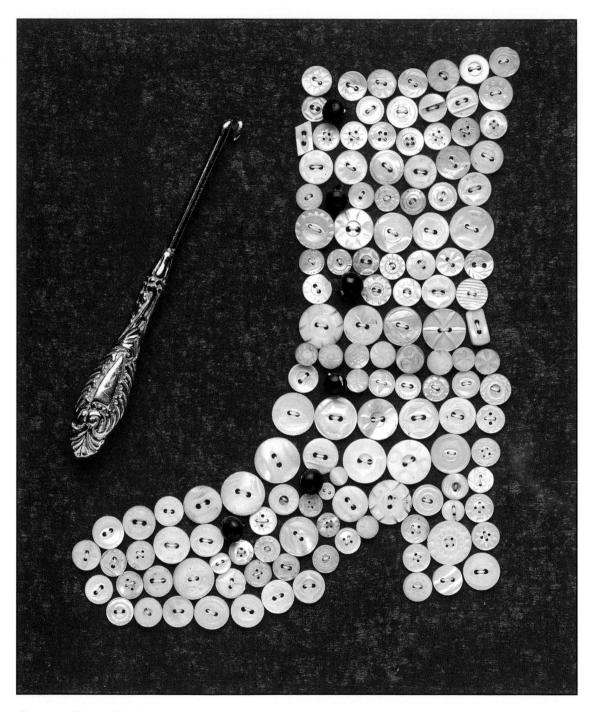

Courtesy of Lynne Mead

A decorative way to use small pearls and shoe buttons.

It's fun to collect things that are related to buttons.
Antique postcards with button faces.

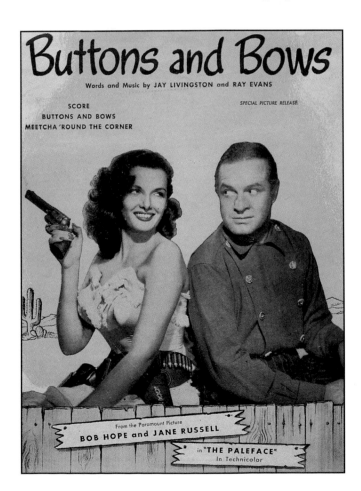

I'm always on the hunt for song titles with the word
"button" in them. I wonder how many are out there?

The National Button Society was organized
in 1938.

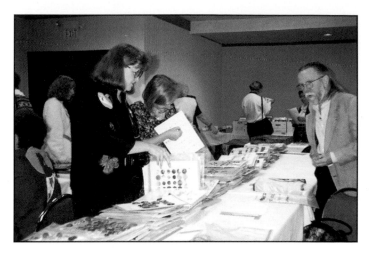

Gee! These women are always hogging the same cards of buttons I want to look at!

See, I told you I could smile. But just this once, so you better get it right!

You own the "Skating in Central Park" button!

I might have what you're looking for, if I could just find the card!

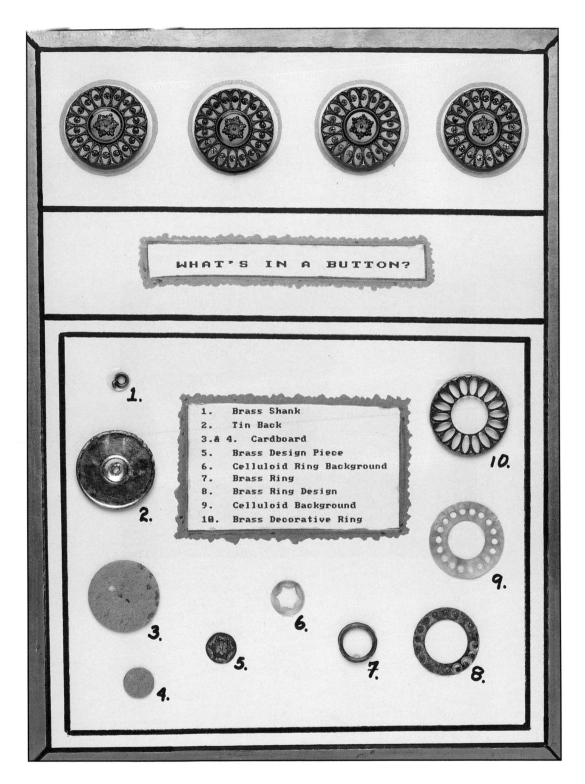

What's In a Button?
Isn't this interesting? This card was made up by my button collecting friend, Lynne Mead.
She carefully took apart one of the old buttons pictured at top.
Look at everything involved in just that one button.

The card reads:

WHAT'S IN A BUTTON?

1.   Brass Shank
2.   Tin Back
3.& 4. Cardboard
5.   Brass Design Piece
6.   Celluloid Ring Background
7.   Brass Ring
8.   Brass Ring Design
9.   Celluloid Background
10.   Brass Decorative Ring

Introduction

Dear Mrs. Wisniewski,

I liked the stuff you showed us and I thank you for the things you brought. The best one's I liked were the moonglows.
from Jeremiah

Thank you for showing us your buttons. I liked the goofy ones.
Katie G.

You have the best buttons in the hole wide world. I love your crystals and underwear buttons.
Joey

I liked your buttons. And I liked the deer ones. Do you no why because I am a deer hunter.
your friend Lucas

Thank you for coming, I want to be in the Button Bug association.
Nicholas

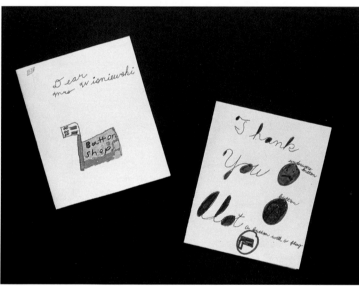

I liked it when you came to school yesterday. I liked the horse buttons the best. Thank you for everything.
your friend Alice

Thank you for sharing your button collection. I liked the flag button the best. I hope you come back in fourth grade.
Sincerely, Jim C.

Thanks for show us your bottons. I'm thinking about gonging to the botton club if my mom and dad let me.
frome brent

Thank you for visiting our class. I'm really interested in the button collection club I would really like to begin a collection but first I need the address and phone number. I am very interested in it I hope I can join the club.
Love, Jesse

Out of all the programs I've given for historical societies and civic groups my favorite one was for my son Tyler's third grade class. Above are notes the children wrote on handmade cards, thanking me for showing some of my buttons to them.

Modern Glass

Throughout this section the term "modern glass" is referring to all glass buttons made after 1918.

Before World War I, Gablonz, in what was then Bohemia, well known for its glass factories, was already producing buttons for export. At the end of World War I Gablonz became part of the new Czechoslovakia. Though still producing buttons, in 1938 parts of Czechoslovakia were annexed to Germany and in 1945 to Russia. Due to their country's economical and political strife they lost their largest customers, the United States. Many of the Jewish factory owners and workers fled 300 miles to start a city called New Gablonz. By the early 1950s the export of glass buttons to the United States was again flourishing. This success continued for about 15 years and by the mid-1960s only 10–15% of the glass factories were still producing buttons. Due to the expense of glass button production and the influx of plastic buttons, their reign in the glass button industry had come to an end!

Transparent glass buttons from the 1930s and 40s
made in Germany, Austria, and Czechoslovakia.
Extra large. $3.00. Others. $.50 – 2.00.
(Shown smaller than actual size.)

*Moonglow leaf realistic,
medium. $8.00.*

*This is a gorgeous example of a precision inlay,
foil backed glass in glass. Large size.
Ca. 1950s. $8.00.*

*Modern black glass with
gold luster. $7.00.*

*Modern black glass with
gun-metal luster. $8.00.*

These modern glass buttons from the mid 1930s to the early 1960s show the variety of paint trims, gold and silver lusters, use of rhinestones, and glass construction techniques so commonly found on buttons from this time period. $2.00 – 4.00 each.

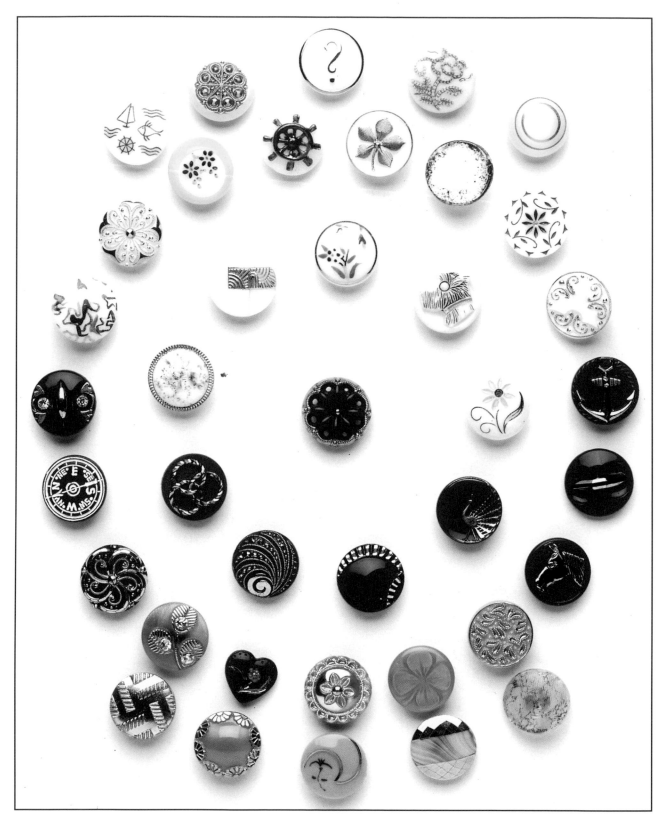

Modern glass, mid 1930s to early 1960s. $2.00 – 3.00 each.

Modern glass, 1930s – 1960s. $1.00 – 3.00 each.

A card of modern blue glass buttons. $1.50 – 3.50 each.

Modern glass from the 1930s, all have the Art Deco influence. $2.00 – 4.00 each.

Little Red Riding Hood, molded blue glass with paint trim. $4.00.

Aurora Borealis from late 1950 – early 1960s.
Small, $2.00 – $3.00. Medium, $4.00 – 6.00.
Far right white button is a moonglow with aurora luster.

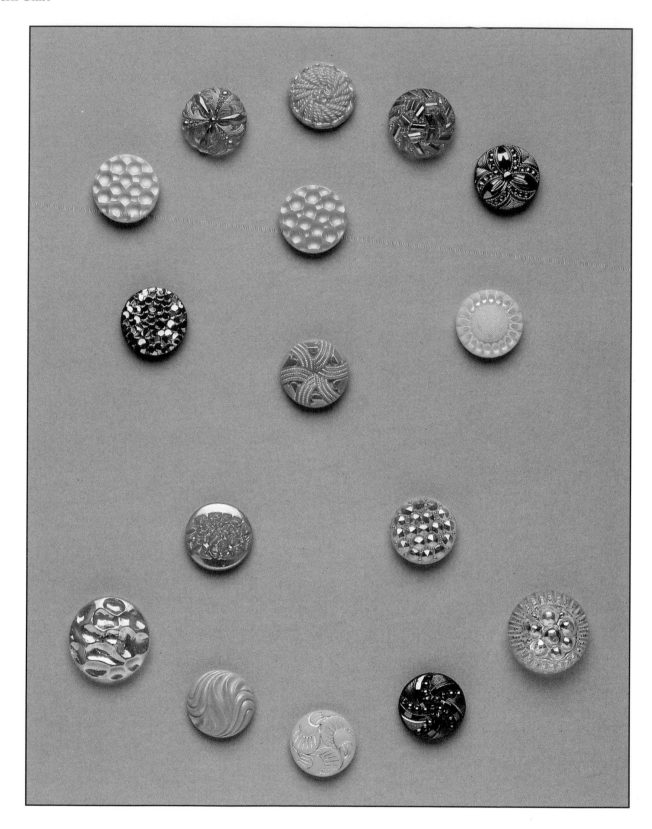

More Aurora Borealis.
Small. $2.00 – 3.00.
Medium. $4.00 – 6.00.

For convenience these glass ball buttons were photographed together. There are examples of old (pre-1918) and modern (post 1918). All have either a metal loop shank or metal loop shank and plate. $2.00 – 4.00.

Two-piece Czechs have intaglio molded tops which were filled in with paint and glued to a glass shank. This hand-done work was probably delicate and time consuming, 1920s – late 1930s. Flowers. $2.00. Golfer. $4.00. (Shown slightly larger than actual size.)

Painted backs. These examples are also painted on intaglio backs, but the button and shank are of one-piece glass construction. Pre-WWII. Small $2.00. Medium $5.00.

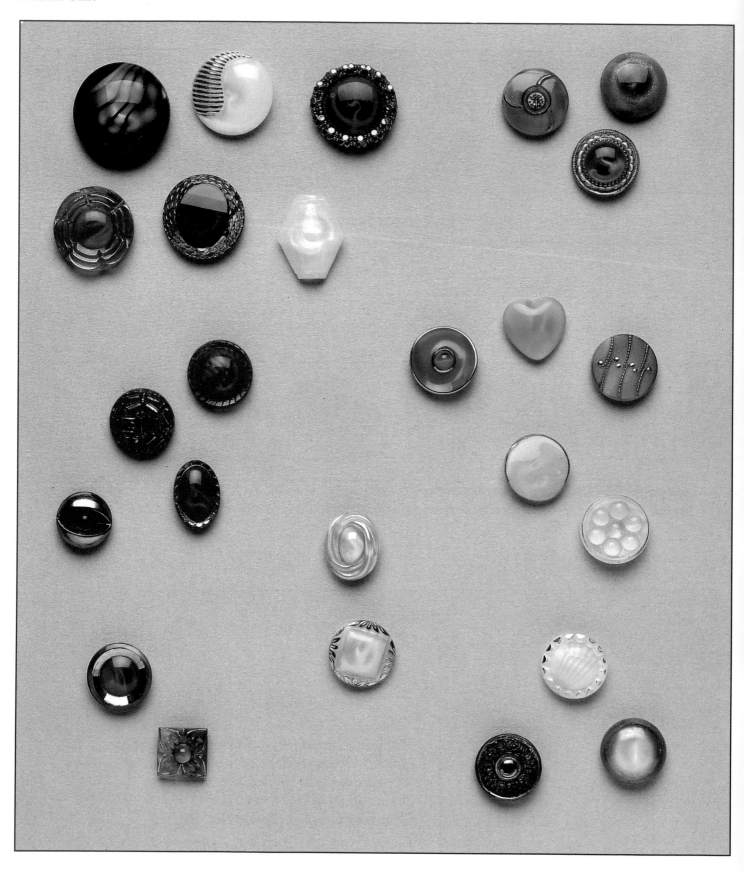

Assorted moonglows.
Medium size. $4.00 − 8.00 (striped). Small size. $2.00–4.00.
Far right: green/white. $6.00.

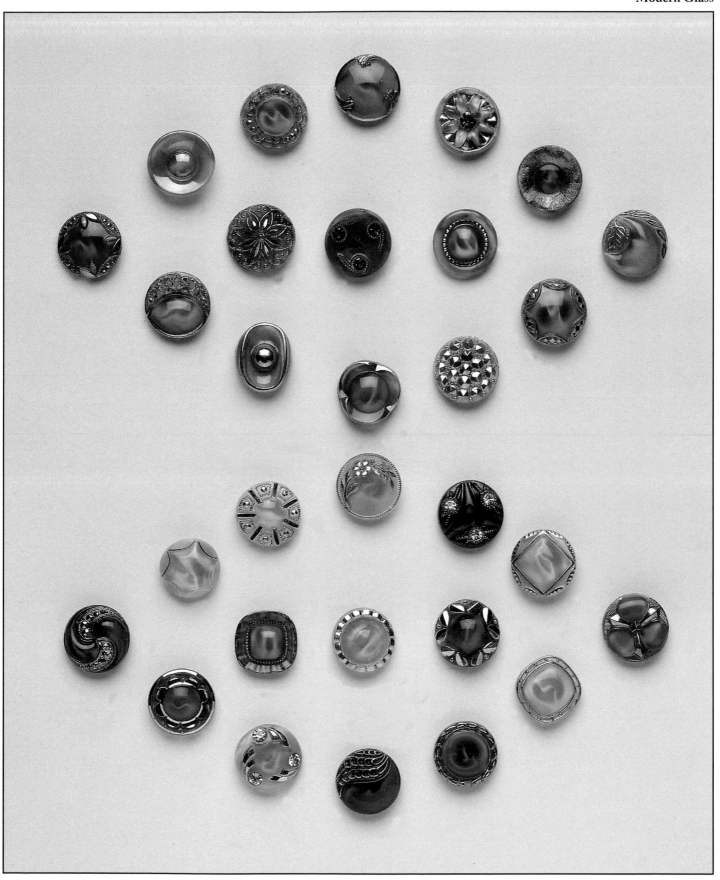

Pink and blue moonglows.
Small (most). $2.00 – 3.00.
Colored stones, modified square and facetted tops. $3.00 – 4.00.

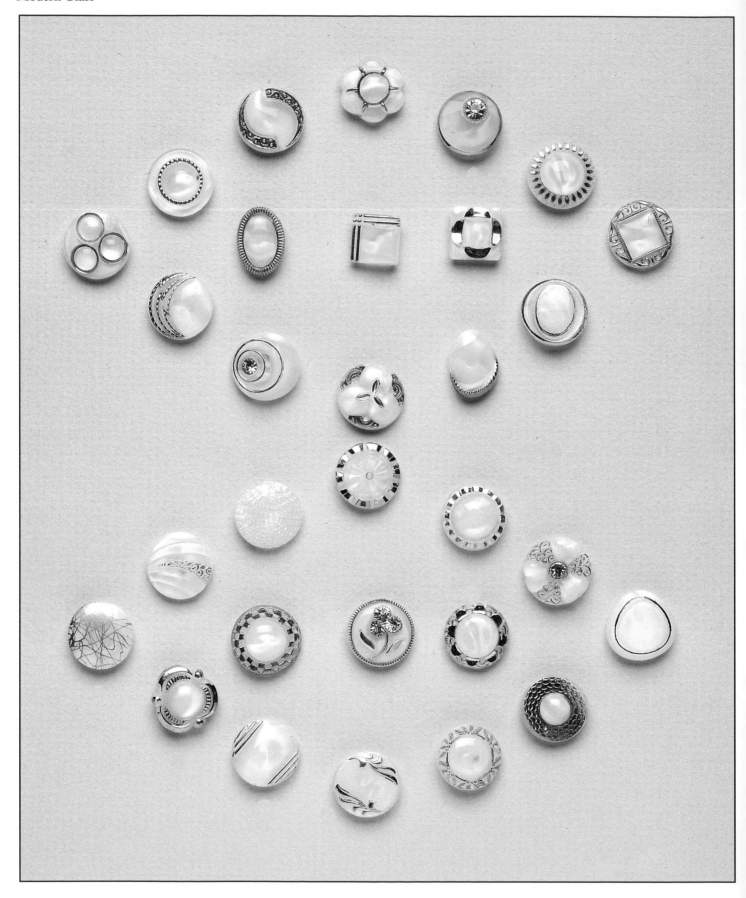

White moonglows.
Small. $2.00. Unusual examples. $3.00 – $4.00.

Modern Paperweights

Here are three examples of John E. Gooderham paperweights. He is well respected throughout the button community. The middle button is especially nice with the double overlay which has been cut and looks like narrow eye slits, with a gold foil horse in the center. He has made paperweight buttons for collectors since 1976 and continues to this day.
$25.00. $75.00. $25.00.

Peter Ben was a paperweight button maker from New Jersey. He was about 70 years young when he started making buttons in the mid-1960s and stopped in the early 1970s. Though they are not high quality, detailed paperweights, they are still very collectible. Heavy round iron shanks pushed in the base with no swirls.
$8.00 – 10.00.

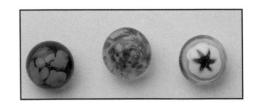

Black glass paperweight by Terry L. Russell of Michigan, ca. 1991. $12.00.

Winfield Rutter made paperweight buttons from the early 1940s to late 1950s. A technique that Rutter used involved different colored layers of glass at the base, that are only noticeable if you look at the side of the button. The three examples shown have sturdy iron shanks pushed in the back. $25.00 – 30.00.

Francis Xavier Weinman, paperweight button maker from the early 1940s to the 1950s. Colored bases scattered with gold stone flecks. Small eyed, iron or brass wire shanks were turned in the glass leaving swirl marks. Top $7.00
Bottom (medium size). $18.00.

Dorothy Hansen of Michigan made paperweight buttons from the early 1970s until the early 1980s. Her "H" signature cane is by the tail of the fish. Dome-shaped cap with hand-formed heavy brass wire shank. Her husband Ronald was known for his desk paperweights. Her son Robert started making paperweight buttons in the early 1970s and continues to do so today. $25.00.

Paperweight button by Robert Hansen, 1996. $30.00.

Mrs. Gooderham, 1982–1987. $20.00.

Theresa Rarig made ceramic buttons but it wasn't until the early 1960s that she made paperweight buttons. Mrs. Rarig's buttons were molded and not built like your true paperweights. Sulphide head on orange base, cemented on metal shank. $30.00.

Lee McMurtry, ca. 1970s. Large, iron, pig-tail shank. A tiny "M" scratched on the back. $35.00.

William Irio, began making buttons in the late 1960s. This is one of his simpler designs, but he also made set-ups of millefiori canes and fruit. Sturdy brass wire shank. $25.00.

Thura Erickson of Massachusetts, made paperweight buttons from 1945 to early 1960s. His paperweights are of the highest quality. Large eyed, thin wire shanks. Two examples of his flower paperweights. $85.00 – 100.00.

Courtesy of Irma Vajda.

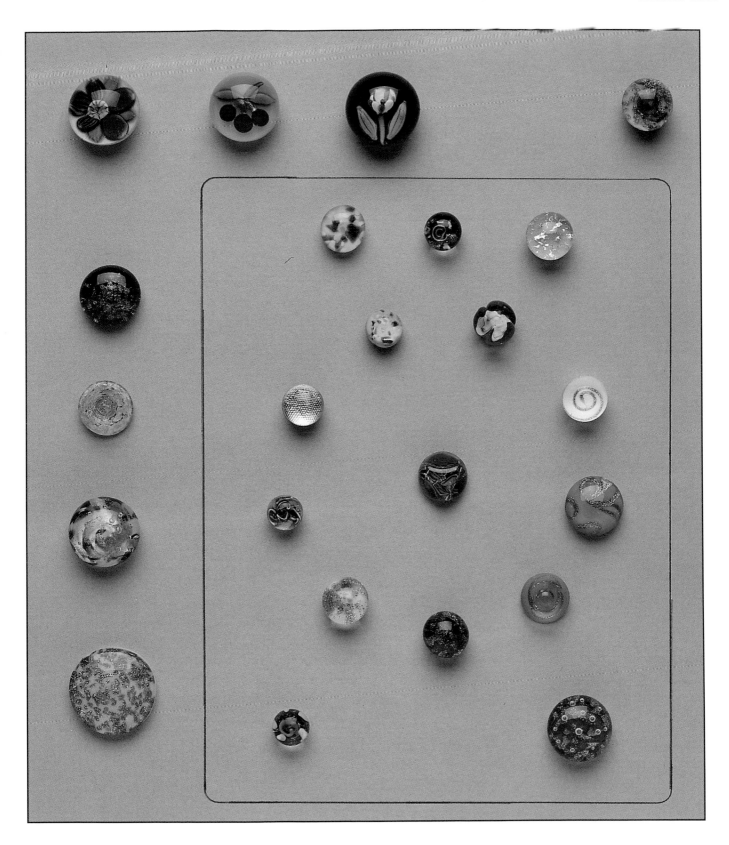

Paperweights.
Top row: 1 – 3) Robert Hansens. $30.00 ea. 4) Winfield Rutter. $30.00.
Left row: All four are Weinman's. $10.00 – 18.00.
Right group: An assortment of mostly modern and a few old paperweights. $6.00 – 15.00.

Bee, ca. 1996. $130.00.   *Cat, ca. 1995.*
$12.00.

Since 1990 William C. Stokes of Blue Flame Studios in Bellingham, WA, has been making lampworked glass paperweight buttons for collectors. Will also does lampworked glass beads and has been a featured artist, guest speaker, and teacher on his lampworked glass techniques.

Unlike the other modern paperweight buttons which were principally made for button collectors, these paperweights were sold in department and fabric stores for use on clothes. Most of them date from the 1920s – 1930s, but many believe they were also made prior to WWI. $7.00. (Shown smaller than actual size.)

Modern black glass with gold luster, 1940s – early 1960s. $2.00 – 4.00 each.

Modern black glass with silver luster, late 1930s – 1950s. $2.00 – 3.00 each.

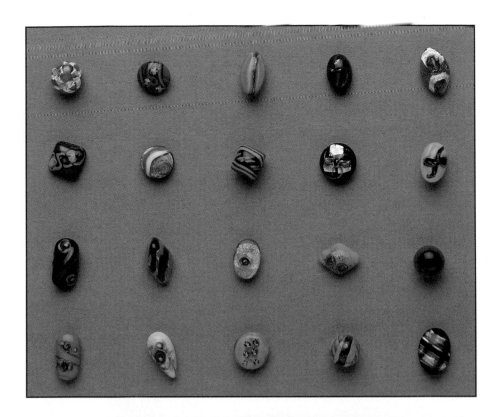

All of these Czechoslovakian glass buttons have the four-way metal box shank.
Several have thread grooves which would be classified as old (pre-1918) and the
remaining with no thread grooves would be modern (after 1918).
Pictured are paperweight and non-paperweight Czechs.
Top photo $3.00-5.00. Bottom photo $4.00 – 10.00.

Charm string glass. A generic term for this type of button. The contrasting color on five of the buttons is called glass overlay trim, ca. 1840 - 1870s. $4.00 each.

Kaleidoscopes. These transparent-top buttons have painted or foil designs on the backside and are cemented to a large metal shank plate. They tend to be fragile. The smooth rounded tops are $10.00 – 15.00. The odd-shaped molded or frosted tops are $15.00 – 20.00. In the top row, the last button is a rare paperweight kaleidoscope. $85.00. These are ca. 1840s–1870s.

Painted backs. Incised molded back, which is filled with paint and glows through the body of the button, ca. 1840 - 1870s. $4.00.

Rosette shanks. This term refers to the design of the metal shank. It is divided into six segments. These glass vest buttons show the quality of workmanship done by the glassworkers of Gablonz in the late 1800s to early 1900s. $3.00 – 5.00 each.

Radiants. Transparent glass buttons which have tiny drops of glass at the shank or on the ribbed underside which allows the colored glass to shine through, ca. 1840s - 1870s. $12.00 – 15.00.

Black glass with silver luster. Bible. $5.00. Girls tossing hoops. $15.00.

Custard Glass. $5.00. Caramel Glass. $4.00. True Slag. $5.00.

This small black glass button with gold luster portrays a knife, fork, and spoon. Collectors call this pictorial objects, formerly termed inanimate. $7.00.

Milk glass with a molded fly, painted black and gold. $8.00.

Owl's face in black glass. Swirl back, loop shank. $5.00.

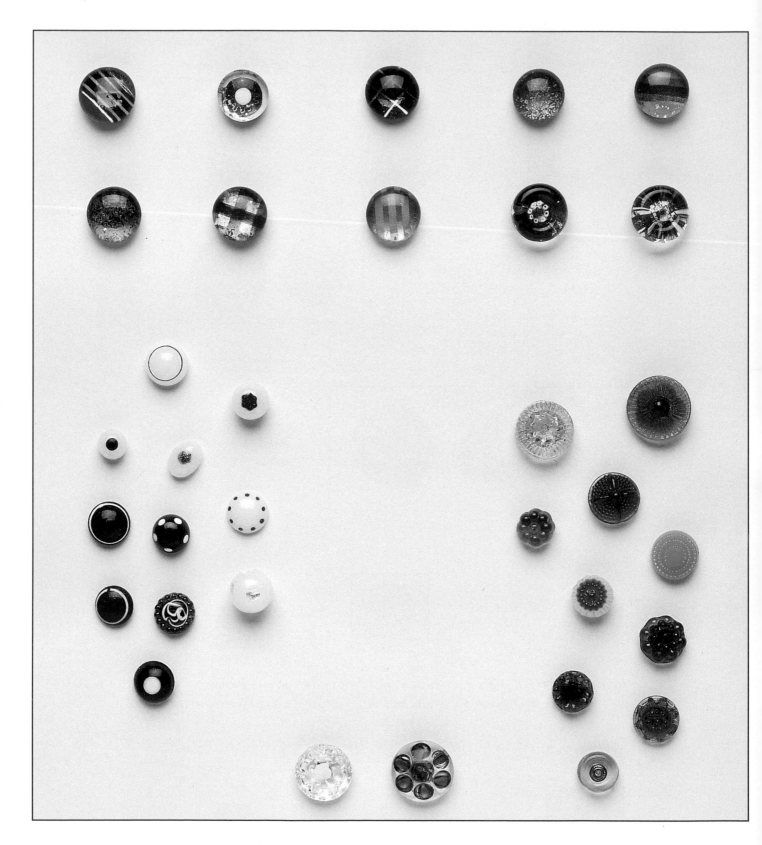

Row 1 and 2: Kaleidoscopes. $10.00 – 15.00.
Left group: Charm string. $2.00 – 4.00.
Right group: Charm string. $2.00 – 4.00.
Bottom group: Radiants. $10.00 ea.

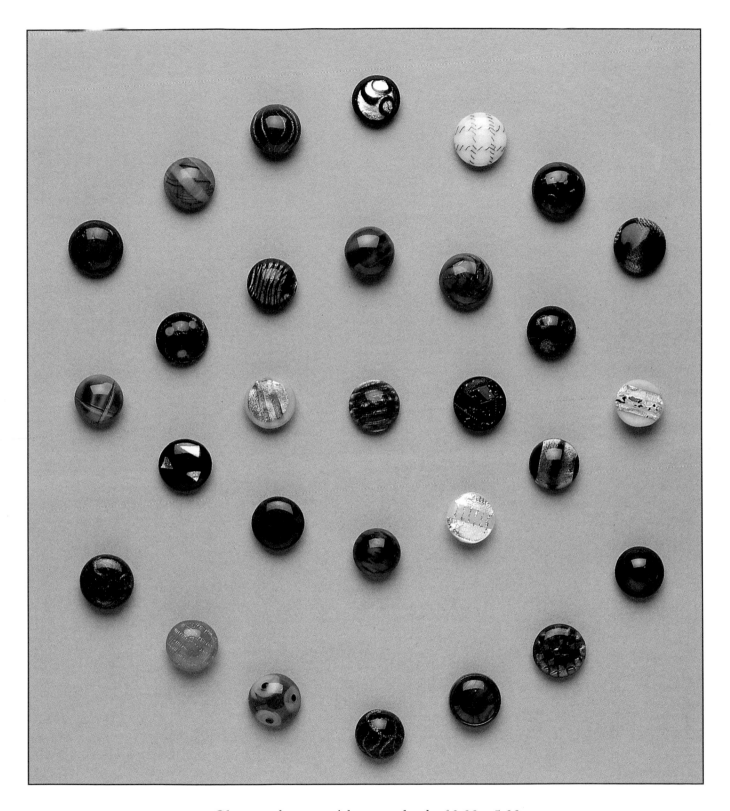

Glass vest buttons with rosette shanks. $3.00 – 5.00.

"Victorian" is the word collectors use for this type of button. They are of opaque or transparent glass with incised or raised line designs that are painted or lustered. They are in white or colored glass (not black). They are from the late 1800s – early 1900s, and have four-way box or two-way hump shanks. $5.00 – $8.00.

*Tortoise glass. Bear claw design.
Metal loop shank and plate. $20.00.*

*Lacy glass. A highly detailed molded glass button with paint applied to the backside and covered in either black or silver paint. Shanks found on lacy glass are four-way metal box and two-way metal hump. Finding these in very good or excellent condition can be a very expensive pursuit.
Small – Large medium size.
Top, 1. $7.00 2. $15.00
3. $15.00 4. $35.00 5. $60.00.
(Shown slightly smaller than actual size.)*

A card of old paperweight buttons made in the same manner as desk paperweights. To qualify as a paperweight there must be a base, set-up, and cap. The base is the bottom of the button. The set-up is the main decoration which includes foil pieces, goldstone, air bubbles, and various glass cane decorations. The base and set-up are then enclosed or topped by clear or transparent colored glass called the cap. All of these old paperweight buttons have wire loop shanks. $8.00 – 15.00 each. Foil butterfly. $18.00.

Black glass with impressed floral design and dull finish background. $5.00.

Running boar. Black glass with brass rim, deeply set loop shank and plate. $25.00.

Flat glass disc with white metal escutcheon lady's head. $15.00.

This button has over sixty individual pieces of black glass that are cemented to a pierced metal framework. $18.00.

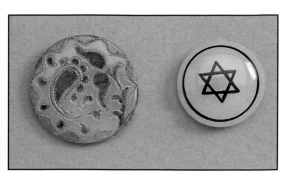

Opaline with paisley design. $10.00. Clambroth six-pointed star. $5.00.

Miscellaneous small black glass pictorials.
$3.00 – 5.00.

Assorted shapes in black glass. $5.00 – 8.00.

Black glass with silver luster, shanks include loop shank and plate,
self-shank, and four-way metal box with thread grooves. $4.00 – 6.00.

Black glass with iridescent luster. Metallic compounds were brushed onto the button and fired at high temperatures fusing it to the glass. Calling these carnival glass is incorrect, since their originality pre-dates this glassware. A variety of subjects from animals and insects to flowers, buildings, and people can be found on these lovely iridescent buttons. *Miscellaneous, small size. $5.00 – 8.00.*
Medium house scene. $15.00.
Medium horseshoe. $6.00.

A sampling of different lusters and paint finishes on old black glass. One has a self-shank and the rest have loop shanks and plates. $3.00 – 7.00.

Black glass pictorials: King Harold. $25.00. Hand/Flowers. $8.00. Acorn. $8.00. Pagoda. $15.00.

Two smooth, flat surface black glass buttons painted in fired, polychrome enamels. $5.00.

Black glass buttons with assorted lusters and paint trims. Small size. $3.00 – 8.00.
(Shown slightly larger than actual size.)

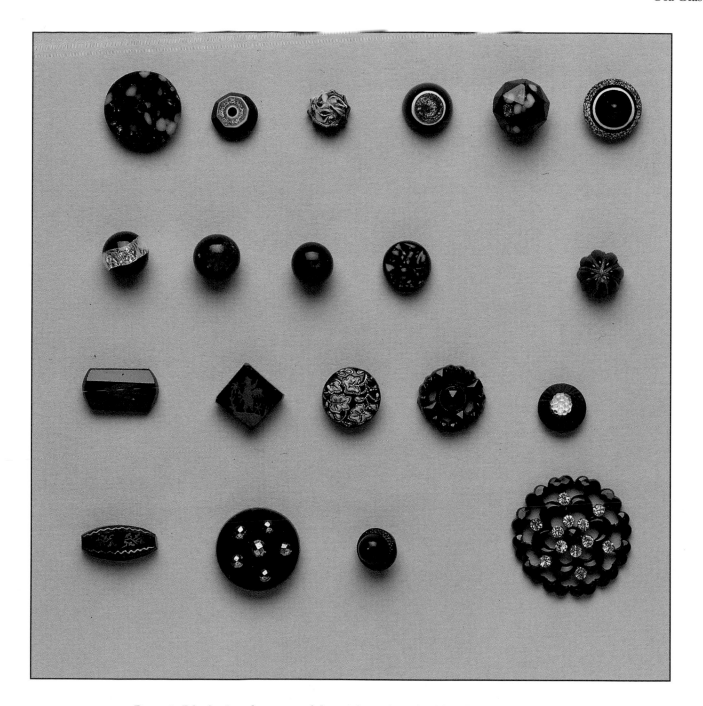

Row 1: Black glass buttons with overlay trim of white glass and goldstone.
The last button is an example of salt overlay trim. $3.00 – 6.00.
Row 2: 1 – 4 are black glass paperweight buttons. $10.00 – 12.00 ea.
The last button is bound by thread and secured under the shank plate. $7.00.
Row 3: Silver painting of bird. $3.00. Scene painted in dull green enamel. $3.00.
Leaves of white enamel and gold luster. $3.50. Pierced. $3.00.
Black glass with a clear berry-shaped top. This type of construction using two separate pieces of
molded glass is called coronet. $3.50.
Row 4: Whistle. $2.00. Black glass with faceted steels that are riveted to a large brass shank plate. $4.00. Black
glass realistic acorn. $5.00.
Black glass pieces glued to an open metal frame with claw set rhinestones. $18.00.

Imitation fabric. A small group of black glass buttons with assorted finishes imitating the fabrics of the Victorian period. $1.00 – 5.00.

*Assortment of old black glass.
Medium-large. $3.00 – 6.00.
Extra large. $15.00.*

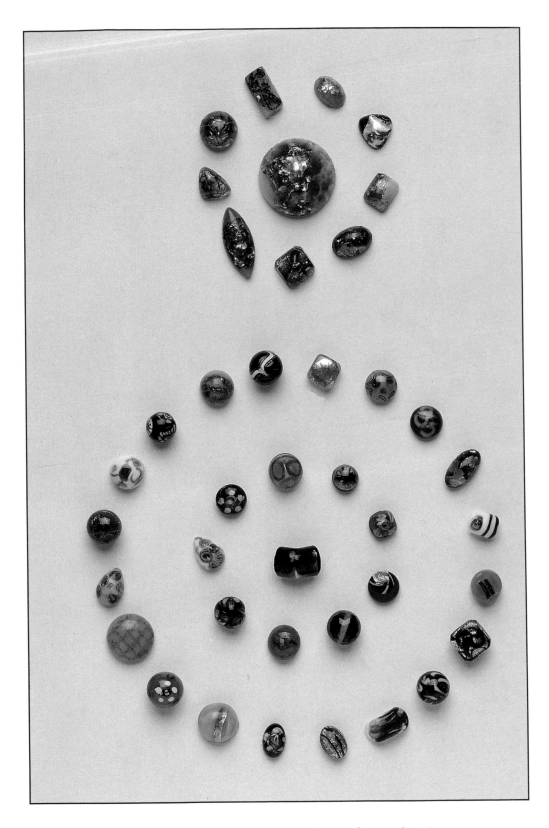

Top group: Poppers, key shank. $2.00. Center. $4.00.
Bottom group: Grooved four-way box shanks and loop shanks with shank plate.
$3.00 – 5.00.

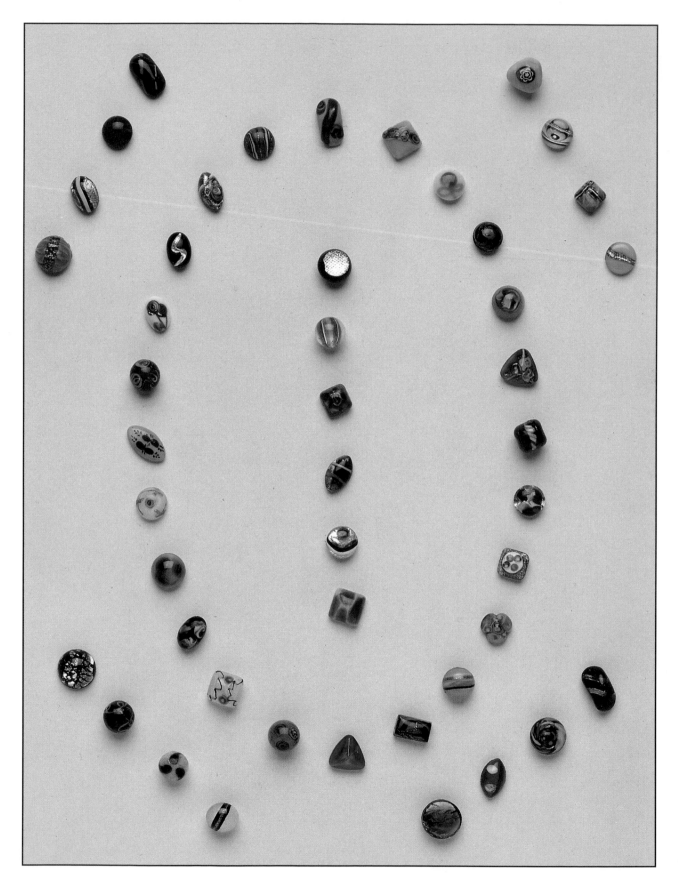

More glass buttons with four-way metal box shanks. Both pre-1918 (old) and post-1918 (modern). $3.00 – 6.00.
(Shown slightly smaller than actual size.)

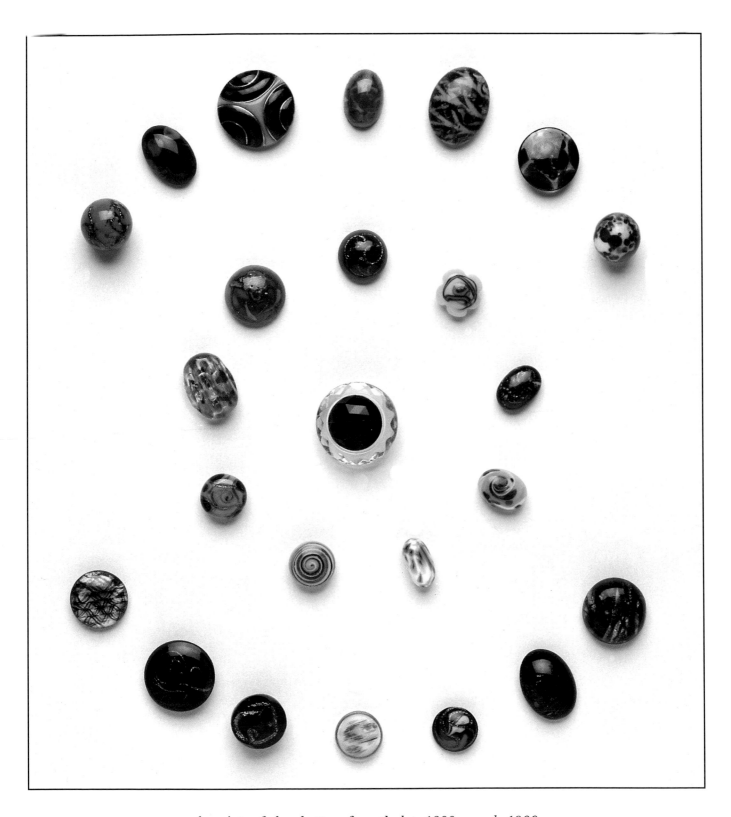

A variety of glass buttons from the late 1800s – early 1900s.
All have metal shanks such as loop, loop and plate, four-way box, and rosette shank.
A few may cross over into modern (after 1918). $2.00 – 6.00.

All plastics can be grouped in two classifications. Casein, celluloid, and lucite are a few examples of thermo-plastics. Bakelite and Catalin are thermoset-plastics.

Thermo-plastics can be heated and softened over and over again to a workable state.

Thermoset-plastics once molded cannot be softened by heat and cannot be remolded. This is where the red-hot needle test is important in determining Bakelite and Catalin from other plastic buttons. Using a propane torch heat a needle until it is glowing bright red. Touch the back of the button, if it goes in or smokes it is thermo-plastic. If the needle leaves a very tiny mark (usually noticeable by using your fingernail) it is Bakelite or Catalin. On the lighter colored buttons it will leave a minuscule brown dot. For the needle test it is very important to use something that gets the needle very hot (not a lighter or candle). A very technical test is the only way to tell Catalin from Bakelite, therefore button collectors classify all thermoset plastics as Bakelite.

Note: All buttons listed in this book as Bakelite have passed the red-hot needle test.

Stamped metal escutcheon of Oriental man on Bakelite. $20.00.

Oriental scene on celluloid. $20.00.

Various types of construction using celluloid. $3.00 – 8.00.

Thin celluloid disc with a pierced brass escutcheon loop shank and plate. $6.00.

Assorted celluloid. $4.00 – 20.00.
(Shown smaller than actual size.)

Reverse carved and painted
lucite button. $7.00.

One-piece celluloids, 1930s. $12.00 each.

Ladies' coat buttons made of Bakelite with black glass centers.
One with gold luster and one with gold colored paint. $6.00.

Imitation tortoise shell. The mitten is plastic and the rest are Bakelite.
From top: $2.00, $7.00, $5.00, $10.00, $12.00.

Imitation tortoise shell plastic and Bakelite.
Pineapple. $2.00. Coin Head. $10.00. Carmen Miranda. $15.00. Center. $8.00. Others. $4.00 – 6.00.

Peanuts and cartoon characters, plastic, 1980s. $1.50 each.

These little plastic buttons are called "snap-togethers." Collectors everywhere are going crazy for them. The majority are imported from France, Germany, Japan, and several other countries. The bottom button is an example of one snapped apart, it is of two-piece construction. The top left Mickey Mouse is of three-piece construction. Ca. 1990s. Pumpkins. $1.00. Felix. $1.50. All others. $3.00.

Tight tops.
A celluloid covering extends over the edge and secures to the metal back. $1.00 – 2.00.

Assorted plastics.
Large fruit plate. $7.00. Bakelite bow. $8.00. Cat face. $6.00. Others. $1.00 – 4.00.

Celluloid overlays.
Thin layers of celluloid were applied to a thicker celluloid base.
When the design was cut it revealed the different colored layers. They are very smooth on the sides
and you cannot feel the layers. This differentiates them from laminated types. $2.00 – 4.00.

Bakelite cookie buttons. Small. $1.00 – $2.00 Square. $3.00. Large. $6.00.

Glittering beauties made of Bakelite. $8.00 – 10.00.

Rouge buttons, unscrew the top and find a surprise! The two examples shown here contain rouge, but some have a solid perfume center with the name marked on the back of the button. The cameo head is the same on both types, but the bases and tops come in different colors. They were made by the Colt Firearms Manufacturing Co. in the 1940s. $15.00 each.

Bakelite Scottie dog. $8.0 0 – 10.00.

Small but sensational, pearl Eiffel Tower riveted to a pearl back by two-faceted steels. The date 1889 is the time of the tower's construction and the Paris Exposition. $12.00.

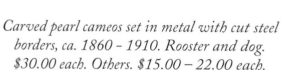

Carved pearl cameos set in metal with cut steel borders, ca. 1860 – 1910. Rooster and dog. $30.00 each. Others. $15.00 – 22.00 each.

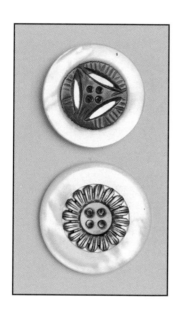

Grey pearl with engraved and painted floral design. $15.00.

Inserts. The white pearl body has a depression and the dark pearl piece is cemented into the cavity. $2.00.

Small pearls with metal trim and one with pearl set in metal. $2.00 – 3.00.

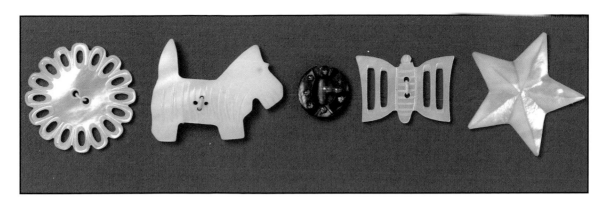

*More pearl realistics. The third button from the left has faceted steel trim
and a brass loop shank attached to the brass buckle hook. $3.00 – 6.00.*

*Pearl owl's face,
late 1800s. $5.00.*

*Pearl realistics,
late 1930s – 1950s.
$1.00 – 2.00.*

Satsuma. These two examples have all the characteristics of the older Satsuma. The shanks have rounded edges and are not glazed. The face of the buttons have gold incrustation and more dots. Pre-WWI. Flower. $15.00. Birds. $45.00.

Modern Satsuma, 1940s - 1950s. Small-mediums $15.00. Large-medium. $25.00.

This red clay pottery button with transparent glaze is backmarked Peru, ca. 1940s. $8.00.

Connecticut Pottery buttons were made between 1825 and 1852 by two pottery firms in Norwalk, Connecticut, and Prospect, Connecticut. They are so much alike that it is difficult to attribute them to a specific factory. Pinhead shank. $7.00.

Kutani porcelain from Japan. Even though they are from the 1950s, they are still very collectible. They do not have the crackled glaze like the Satsuma. This set is the Seven Immortals. $250.00 set.

Prices for photo on page 67:

China buttons were manufactured as early as the 1840s in England, France, and the United States. China stencils were sold up to the 1930s.
1. Small china calicoes. $2.00 – $3.00. 2. Medium calico. $40.00.
3. Calicoes with dark bodies. $7.00. 4. Rimmed calico. $28.00.
5. Assorted chinas. $1.00. 6. Medium hobnail rim. $25.00.
7. China whistles. $5.00. 8. China stencils. $2.00. 9. Square stencils. $3.00.
(Shown slightly smaller than actual size.)

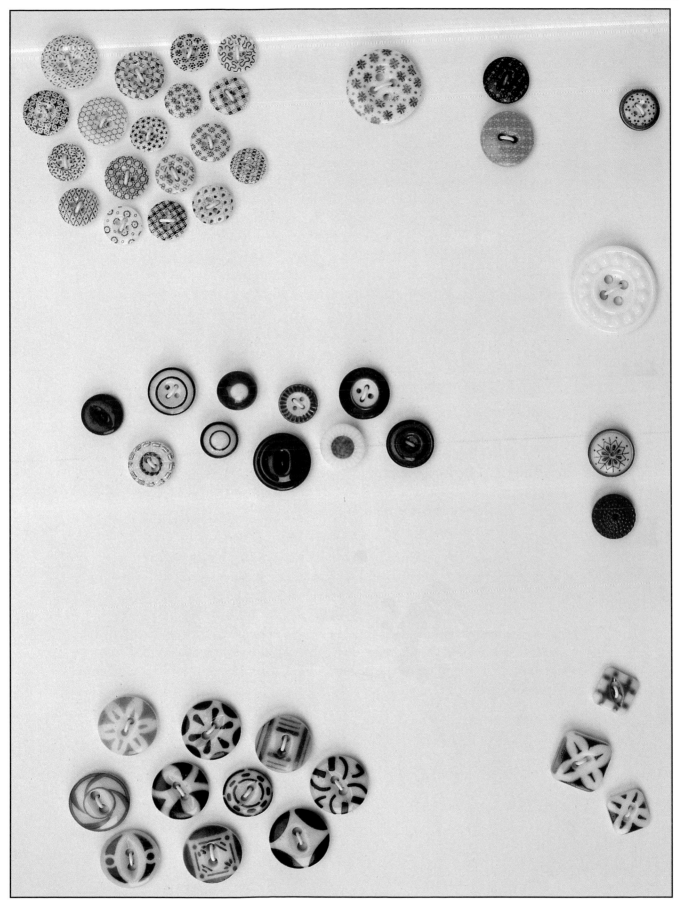

Many collectors specialize by obtaining rare patterns and colors, ones set in metal and rimmed with metal. This is also a category where the saying "the bigger the better" applies. See page 66 for more information.

Picture buttons came onto the scene in the 1860s, by the 1870s they were the height of fashion. This trend continued until about 1915. Picture buttons were manufactured in the United States, Germany, England, and France. The majority of the picture buttons are not backmarked. A few of the backmarks you might find are GESCHUTZT (protected), DEPOSE (registered), and T.W.&W. Paris (Trelon, Weldon & Weil) who were in business from 1814 to 1864. Another French firm you will find is A.P. & Cie (Albert Parent & Co.). Picture buttons mirrored popular plays, fashion trends, commemorative events, and the culture of that day. Studying picture buttons is like being in history class all over again but a lot more fun!

One-Piece Construction: The shank is applied directly to the back of the button, there is no separate rim or separate back.

Two-Piece Construction: This is a button with a front and a separate back. Sometimes the front curves over the edges and holds the back on, or the back curves over the edges toward the front.

Three-Piece Construction: This type consists of the face, rim, and back. The rim holds the three pieces together.

Many of the picture buttons depicting the exact same design can be found in different construction types. Therefore, it does not warrant explaining every button in this chapter, most of them are self-explanatory as to whether they are brass, silvered brass, or tinted brass.

Animals, Insects & Birds

Deer in woods. $14.00.

Stag, cap, and whip. $25.00.

*Said the spider to the fly!
Stamped and tinted brass.
Brass rim, steel back, and wire
shank. $40.00+.*

*Floppy eared rabbit. Back-
marked "T.W.&W HM Paris."
$8.00.*

*Kittens in a slipper.
$12.00.*

Lion at rest. $8.00.

*Rabbit learning
ABC's, white metal.
$10.00.*

Circus cat, mirror liner
in background. $22.00.

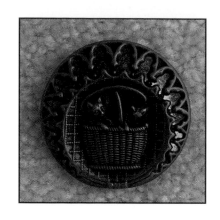

Kittens in a basket,
mirror liner. $75.00+.

Whippet. $8.00.

A dog checking out a rooster
on his house. $10.00.

Dog, silvered brass, backmarked T.W.&W. Paris.
$8.00.

Beehive. $12.00.

What a cute and contented cat! This large oval brass cat button is an Ashlee button. In the mid 1940s button collectors learned that the Ashlee Company had stock from two button firms who had manufactured buttons from the 1870s to the 1930s. Collectors purchased the remaining assembled buttons and quickly requested that buttons be made up from the old unassembled pieces. Therefore, Ashlees are buttons assembled from the mid 1940s to the early, 1950s from old button findings. Notice the white soldering marks, another sign of Ashlee's. Even with that they are still highly collectible. $75.00+. (Slightly smaller than actual size.)

Mountain goat. $18.00.

Bison. $22.00.

*Two nice examples of sporting buttons. Gilt brass and heavy brass backs.
Both are backmarked "Treble Standard/Extra Rich." Most sporting buttons
came six or more to a set depicting different hunting scenes or animals.
I am very fond of the button picturing the shetland pony, not only because of the fine
detail but because it is the same pony I had as a child, named Brownie. Ca. 1850s.
Fox. $10.00. Shetland pony. $18.00.*

*Barn swallow and her babies with
pierced windows and metal mirrored
liner showing through white metal collet.
$16.00.*

*Bird carrying flowers. Stamped
and tinted brass and backed
with velvet. $12.00.*

Bird on brick wall. $10.00.

Bird guarding her nest, great detail, silvered brass. $25.00.

Rooster. At first glance this looks like a two-piece, but it is really of three-piece construction (face, rim, and back). $35.00.

Parrots. Tinted brass, painted metal background. $8.00.

Bird. $10.00.

Brass bird with faceted steel border and tiny steel eye. $12.00.

Lion head. $10.00.

Steeple chase. $15.00.

Bird on a branch. Brass bird on engraved steel background. $6.00.

Architectural Structures & Scenes

Egyptian ruins. $7.00.

Charter Oak. This is said to be an older title, but many collectors still use it. $15.00.

Castle on a rocky promontory. $12.00.

Castle. $10.00.

Old street lamp. $10.00.

Alpine cabin. $10.00.

Italian villa. $10.00.

Children & Children's Stories

The Goose That Laid the
Golden Egg. $16.00.

Hansel and Gretel. $18.00.

Three Peas in a Pod.
$22.00

Sailor boy and anchors.
$16.00.

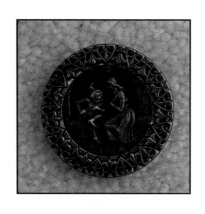

Rumpelstiltskin. $22.00.

Man Friday from the
story Robinson Crusoe.
$22.00.

Now for it or chase of
pleasure. $25.00.

Merlin the Magician at
the cottage door of the
ploughman. $22.00.

Hop o' my thumb. $20.00.

*Brother and sister, silvered brass
with brass rim, steel back and wire
shank. $50.00*

*Playland wash day.
$25.00.*

Little sleeper. $85.00.

*Girl hoop rolling.
$22.00.*

*Fox and the Grapes,
fable. Faceted steel trim.
$15.00.*

*Inno and Nello or The Waits.
$12.00.*

*Child's face in center
of flower. $6.00.*

*Porridge time, one-piece stamped brass.
$6.00.*

Fox and the Stork, fable. Brass with faceted steel border. $15.00.

Red Riding Hood and the Wolf. This button was reproduced in the 1940s and I believe this is one of them. The shank is of white metal. Though it is loose like the older ones, it does not cross at the base like the older one. The black on the back of the button is rougher and when you tap the back with your finger-nail it sounds different than the old backs. $25.00.

Isn't she cute, this little miss and her fancy clothes. Silvered brass front with a white metal back and stiff loop shank. Modern, maybe 1940s. $40.00.
(Shown slightly smaller than actual size.)

Kate Greenaway is a well-known children's illustrator from the late 1800s. This button is titled Miss Patty. It was made in the 1940s using old dies. It is what collectors call one of The 13. A dealer had 13 different buttons made from old dies. For competition purposes they must be classed with moderns. Brass with black lacquer coating. $25.00.

The Little Red Hen. One-piece brass with cut-steel trim. $35.00.

These are old Kate Greenaway buttons, but some were also made in the 1940s in France with old dies. $10.00 – 20.00 each.

Couples

Paul and Virginia. $15.00.

*Radlauf the Miller.
$15.00.*

*Goatherd's romance.
$16.00.*

*Two different examples
of John Alden proposing
to Priscilla. $15.00.*

*John Alden and Priscilla, very large.
$35.00.*

*Lucy and Edgar. Can also be
classed as an opera $25.00.*

*Francesca and Paolo.
$20.00.*

*Arthur Bonnicastle and
Millie Bradford. $25.00.*

Cupids, Cherubs, Putti & Gnomes

*Putto or Putti — chubby child-like
figure, partially clothed or nude, no wings.*

*Cherub — chubby child-like figure partially
clothed or nude with wings.*

*Cupid — partially clothed or nude and must have a torch, a quiver, or a bow. Only
one winged figure shown. Cupids are usually winged, but there are a few exceptions.*

*Putto at the fountain.
$10.00.*

*Putto and young woman at
well. $15.00.*

*Cherub with mask
frightening dog. $25.00.*

*Cupid standing in shell
boat, quiver under sail.
$16.00.*

*This very detailed silvered brass button has been known as
pensive cherub. Due to the wings, his bow across his lap, and
closed eyes I think Cupid nods off would be more suitable.
$40.00.*

Cupid kissing Psyche, his beloved. A beautiful silvered brass button with brass rim and back, self shank. $50.00. (Note: Following the mythological story, I decided to still call him Cupid even though a quiver, torch, or bow are not pictured.)

Cherub riding a seahorse. $6.00.

Cherub sailing in a swan boat. $25.00.

Puck. $8.00.

Cupid finds a victim. $10.00.

Imp of Pain. $22.00.

Cupid and Erato. $18.00.

Putto at the column. Common. $8.00.

Cupid at rest. Common. $8.00.

This could be a child, and in the 1940s it was called Jack the Giant Killer watering his beanstalk. But since his bare bottom in showing maybe it's a putto watering plants. $6.00.

Egyptian

The Gardens at Karnak
$8.00.

Cleopatra. $8.00.

Funeral mask. $18.00.

Cleopatra and the Asp.
$12.00.

Sphinx. $3.00 each.

Egyptian queen.
$5.00.

Egyptian head. $6.00.

Queen Zakuta, one-piece brass.
$15.00.

Fabulous Animals

Dragon with wood background.
$25.00.

Wyvern. $5.00.

Dragon. $4.00.

Dragon. $5.00.

Gargoyle heads. $8.50.

Dragon. $5.00.

Men

Indian chief. $35.00.

Friar Tuck? $55.00.

Roland. $15.00.

Theodore Roosevelt hunting rhino. It has been said this was made up from metal findings not related to buttons. Some collectors and dealers I've talked to believe they are genuine buttons. Whatever they are, the workmanship is good and would make a fine addition to any collection. The other two similar buttons are Roosevelt hunting lion and Roosevelt hunting elephant. $20.00.

Stanley and Livingston, silvered brass and painted metal background, back-marked "Geschutzt." $22.00.

Tammerlane or Timour the Lame, descendant of Genghis Kahn. $15.00.

$12.00.

$15.00.

*Two buttons depicting Blondel, poet
and songster to Richard I of England.*

*Cellini, Italian sculptor.
$25.00.*

*Gentleman (?)
Probably King Charles I of
England. $18.00.*

Drinking at the inn. $40.00+.

Charles I of England. $15.00.

*Made around 1910 for children's
clothing, after Perry went to the
North Pole. $15.00.*

Mythological

*Pax (peace), Bellum (war), Apollo, four races of the world,
one is hidden behind the world.
$3.00. $3.00. $3.00. $2.00.*

Apollo. $10.00.

Medusa. $30.00.

*Catherine the Great as
Minerva. $32.00.*

Minerva. $15.00.

Pegasus. $25.00.

Bacchanal girl, a loyal follower of Bacchus, god of wine. $12.00.

Mars, god of war. $10.00.

Aeneas and Charon. $32.00.

King Harold. This brass button with a wooden background is backmarked "A.P. & Cie, Paris." Also has been called Wodin and Lohengrin. $28.00.

Hector. $10.00.

Neptune riding the waves. $6.00.

Neptune, wooden background. $12.00.

Opera & Theatre

The Trumpeter of Sackingen.
$18.00.

Punchinello and Harlequin.
$7.00.

Pierrot and Pierrette, common.
$12.00.

Gunther and Brunnhilde,
mirrored liner. $25.00.

Mary Tudor. $12.00.

Oberon and Titania.
$25.00.

Canio. $27.00.

Arrival of Lohengrin. $16.00.

Oriental

$20.00. $24.00.

Two examples of Katisha from the opera Mikado. Many of these Orientals can also be classified in the opera and theatre category.

Madame Chrysanthème. $18.00.   *Madame Butterfly. $35.00.*

Two examples of Yum-Yum. The button on the left is what we collectors call one piece. It is stamped out in brass and does not have a separate back piece like the button to the right. $16.00. $12.00.

Chinaman with
umbrella, one piece.
$7.00.

Miscellaneous small Orientals.
$2.00 – 3.00 each.

Peep-Bo and Pitti-Sing,
sister's of Yum-Yum.
$8.00.

Oriental man. $12.00.

Plant Life

Lily of the valley or bell
flower. $4.00.

Floral, tinted brass, cut-steel
trim, mirror liner. $5.00.

Ivy leaves on a fence. This extremely
large brass button with faceted steel
trim is called a handkerchief corner
button. Trying to assemble a card of
these is quite difficult. $50.00.

Flower, tinted brass.
$4.00.

Religious

Why hath Thou forsaken me. This is the name I have given this button. I could not find any documented title. Jesus was not portrayed very often on buttons. The detail is exceptional. Silvered brass front wraps around to the back which is brass with a self shank. $200.00.

Eliezer at the Well. $12.00.

Charlemagne and the warning angel. Stamped brass and painted metal background. $14.00.

Two monks relaxing. Stamped and tinted brass, two piece. $15.00.

The flight of Mohammed from Mecca, brass with purple tint. $10.00.

Sports & Transportation

This is a silvered brass button with brass rim, steel back, and wire shank. I think "touring the countryside" would be a nice name. $65.00.

Early auto. $8.00.

Early auto. $8.00.

Sailboat in a shell. One piece, stamped and tinted brass. $18.00.

Coin-type button of one-piece brass. $10.00.

Women

Jeanne Hachette or Jean La Hache, French heroine. $22.00.

Waving goodbye. $18.00.

Lalla Rookh, Princess of India. $16.00.

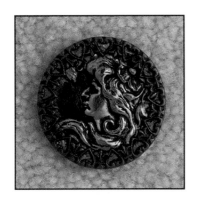

Art Nouveau woman. $35.00.

Art Nouveau woman. $35.00.

Playing mandolin. $16.00.

Girl archer on balcony. $12.00.

Women seated among bamboo branches, wooden background. $18.00.

Empress Elizabeth of Austria. $16.00.

Duchess of Devonshire. $30.00.

Sarah Lennox at Holland House. $16.00.

Fishermaiden with net. $6.00.

Miscellaneous Pictorials

Bonnet, large one-piece brass with engraving. $45.00.

Flag with enamel. $32.00.

Umbrellas. $22.00.

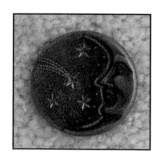

Moon and Haley's Comet, stamped one-piece brass. $5.00.

This heraldic design of the rampant lion is a common button, wooden background. $8.00.

Brushing cobwebs off the moon. $18.00.

Small Picture Buttons

Examples of small picture buttons with faceted steels. $2.00 – 5.00.

An assortment of small size picture buttons, ⅜" to ¾", some of these came in medium, ¾" – 1¼", and large 1¼" and over. $2.00 – 5.00.
(Shown slightly smaller than actual size.)

Falcon huntress. $32.00.   Jaunting carriage. $38.00.   Hymen, god of marriage. $25.00.
Henry of Navarre. $32.00.   Dragon. $9.00.   Gnome watering toadstools. $60.00.
Lion. $4.00.   Rooster. $22.00.   Little Billee. $22.00.   Children playing with puppet. $18.00.
Young man. $8.00.   Can we share? $16.00.   Peacock. $5.00.

The large button (top left) is made of faceted steels, each individually riveted to a metal base. The others are examples of cut steels as trim.
$5.00 – 10.00 each.

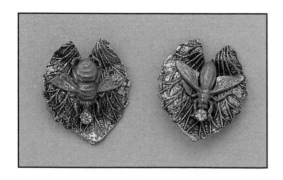

Gold and silver colored metal with brass insects and rhinestone trim, modern (after 1918). $8.00 each.

Japanned brass, engraved.
$2.00 – 3.00 each.

*Pewter,
paisley design. $6.00.*

Assortment of small size pewters. $2.00 – 3.00 each.

*Pewter, two putti fishing.
$10.00.*

Pewter. $4.00.

*Hallmarked sterling silver,
maker's mark of "S.M.L."
(1 o'clock) and essay marks
at 3 o'clock, Birmingham,
1904 – 1905. $25.00.
(Shown slightly smaller
than actual size.)*

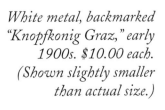

*This brass face with cut-steel
trim is mounted in a steel cup
by pins you can see on the
back. $5.00.*

Pewter. $8.00.

*Tourists to the southwest purchased
buttons to take home. The three examples above are modern, late 1940s –
early 1950s. $5.00 each.*

*White metal, backmarked
"Knopfkonig Graz," early
1900s. $10.00 each.
(Shown slightly smaller
than actual size.)*

The buttons in rows 1 – 4 have faceted steel pieces which are individually riveted in place.
In the last row the buttons combine both stamped pieces and riveted steels.
Row 1: $7.00 – 10.00.   Row 2: $4.00 – 6.00.
Row 3 and 4: $5.00 – 8.00.   Row 5, right and left: $5.00.
Center: $12.00.

Gay 90s or Large Jewels

*The controversy continues on what constitutes a true Gay 90s button. Whether
they are Gay 90s or large jewels, they are still favorites among collectors. I have
included examples of both types, you decide!
Large center button. $40.00. All others. $15.00 – 25.00.
(Shown slightly smaller than actual size.)*

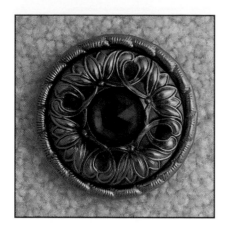

Gay 90s. $26.00.

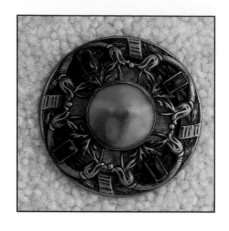

Gay 90s. $38.00.

Intaglio-molded and paint-filled glass tops mounted in metal. $3.00 – 4.00 (cards).

Jeweled waistcoats, ca. 1860 – 1890. $3.00 – 8.00.

Large glass center stone surrounded by cut steels and mounted in metal. $28.00.

Black glass set in a painted metal oval frame. Metal back and brass loop shank. Back-marked "Gesetzlich and Geschutzt." $6.00.

This black glass button with gold luster is mounted in a brass rim and steel back with wire shank, 1880s – 1890s. $10.00.

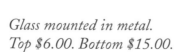

Glass mounted in metal. Top $6.00. Bottom $15.00.

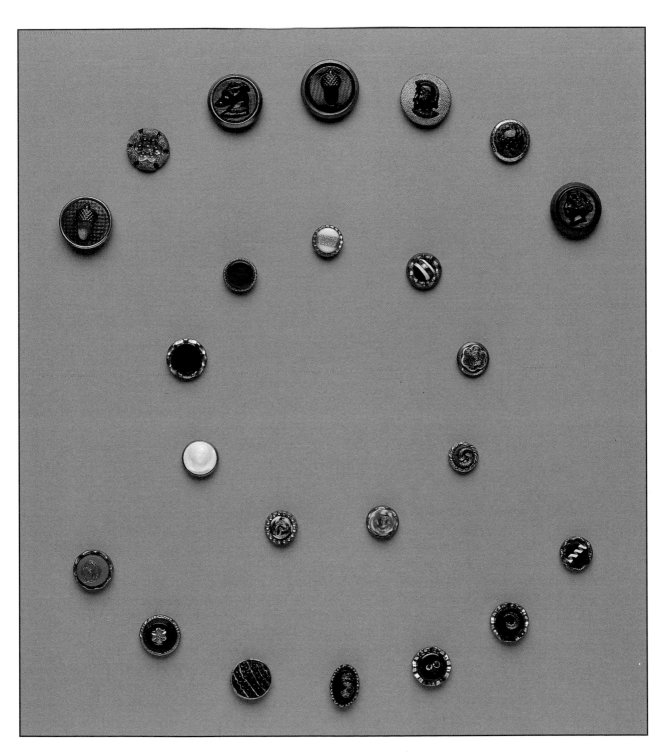

Waistcoat jewels and Victorians. $3.00 – 6.00.

*Old seaman. Gray tinted celluloid with
black lacquered rim, steel back with self-
shank. $75.00+.
(Shown slightly smaller than actual size.)*

*Ivoroids are stamped out of thin sheets of celluloid
which are tinted with various colors such as green,
blue, and yellow, with a large majority in brown
and set in metal, late 1800s. $45.00 - 60.00.*

*Small size ivoroids.
$3.00 each.*

*Lithographs protected with a thin sheet
of celluloid. The dog is very unusual for
this type of button, late 1800s to early
1900s. $30.00. $35.00. $125.00+.*

Pressed wood designs set in metal.
$10.00 – 15.00 each.

Beautiful, yellow molded glass Oriental
woman with fan, Oriental symbols,
and behind her is a brick wall with
flowers. Pierced brass rim and brass
back with wire shank. Possibly lalique
glass from the 1920s. $300.00.

Another gorgeous glass button mount-
ed in metal. The glass is green and
very thick with an iridescent luster on
top. At first glance it looks like a tint-
ed liner where the brass rim starts, but
it is actually the glass itself. Brass rim,
lacquered steel back, and wire shank.
$60.00.

Black glass elephant set in brass,
black lacquered back, self shank.
Great button! $50.00.

Molded white glass lady's head
with blue paint, outer edge of
glass has silver luster, silvered
brass rim, brass back with self-
shank. $18.00.

Glass mounted in metal, late 1800s – early 1900s.
Top row: $7.00 – 10.00.
Inner circle: $3.00 – 5.00.
Bottom row: $5.00 – 15.00.

Top row: Claw-set in silver-plated mountings. Middle button backmarked "Deposé HJ."
Late 1800s - early 1900s. $10.00 – 15.00 each.

Middle row: Cup-set stones.
$3.00 – 5.00 each.

Bottom Row: The first button is plastic with imitation pearls and orange glass stones.
Second button is plastic with rhinestones.
Third button is gold colored metal and rhinestones.
1930 – early 1950s. $4.00 – 7.00 each.

The first button has claw-set strass and saphiret stones mounted in brass with loop shank, late 1800s to early 1900s. $15.00.

Blue glass with goldstone surrounded by rhinestones, set in gold colored metal, loop shank, late 1930s. $7.00.

Rhinestones surrounding a deep pink stone, lacks quality, 1930s or 1940s. $2.00.

Rhinestones with aurora coloring set in soft gold-colored metal, backmarked "ANN," 1950s. $5.00.

Rhinestones set in metal, late 1920s – 1930s. $5.00.

Miscellaneous rhinestone buttons and plastic buttons with rhinestone trim.
Row 1: $7.00 – 10.00.
Row 2: $3.00 – 5.00.
Row 3: $2.00 – 4.00.

One-piece brass and silvered brass with cobalt blue
enamel backgrounds, ca. late 1800s – early 1900s.
Her headdress is representative of an Egyptian
queen, possibly Cleopatra. $40.00 each.

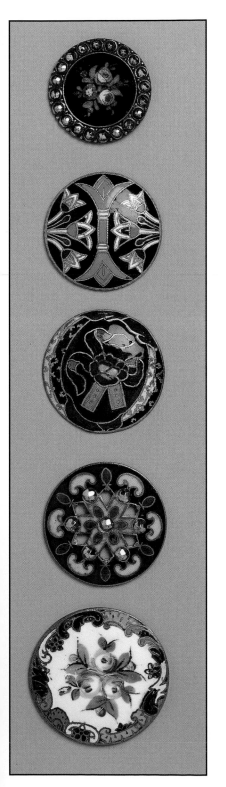

Painted enamel on
brass. $20.00

Assorted shapes.
$7.00 – 10.00 each.

Painted enamel roses on black with faceted steel border. $18.00.

Champlevé enamel, Art Deco style. $30.00.

Champlevé enamel with a flower and ribbon motif. $30.00.

Champlevé on pierced brass with faceted steel trim. $35.00.

Painted enamel roses with a champlevé border. $35.00.

Dome-shaped enamels.
$8.00 – 10.00 each.

A beautiful example of
Bassetaille enamel with painted enamel roses and touches of
gold paint, brass rim, black lacquered back
and loop shank. $40.00.

A grouping of small size
enamels. $5.00 – 8.00.

Enamel on brass with
cut-steel trim border.
$20.00.

Assorted enamels.
$15.00 – 22.00.

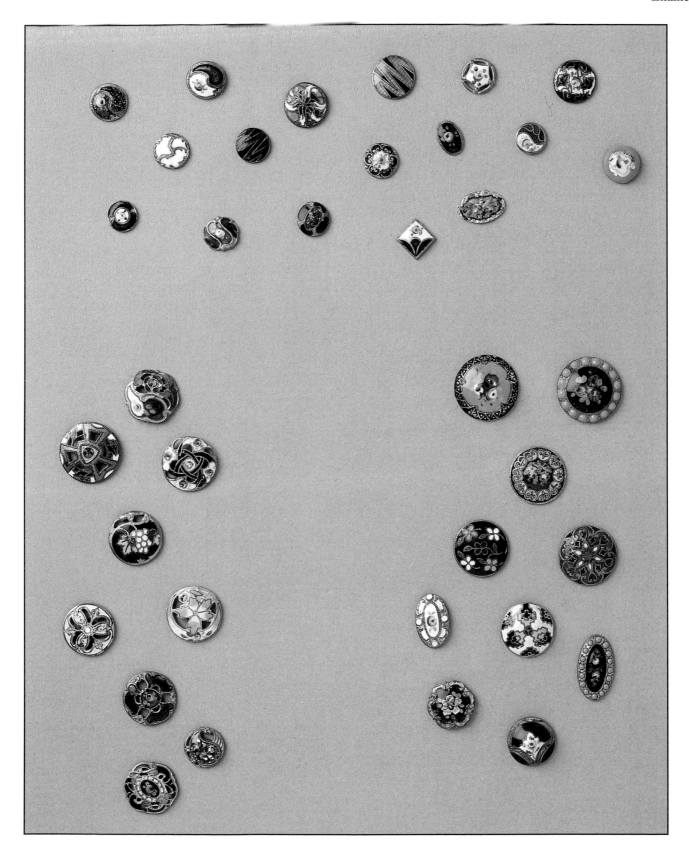

Top group: Diminutive, small enamels. $3.00 – 4.00.
Left group: Pierced small-size enamels. $4.00 – 5.00.
Right group: Small enamels. $4.00 – 7.00.
(Shown slightly larger than actual size.)

Goofies *or* Realistics

Each collector has a preference. My personal choice is goofies for the plastic and glass sets and realistics for the metal, pearl, coconut shell, wood, etc. I do not think of goofies as a negative term for these fun-loving buttons, but a name that reflects their own personality and charm.

Button collector and author, Dorothy Foster Brown came up with this whimsical title in the early 1940s. To quality as a goofy, the button must be in the shape of what it is depicting. There are a few sets like the hunting scenes set that are round, and these are called conventional sets. Most of the glass and plastic goofies on the following pages are from the 1930s – early 1950s from Europe and the United States, unless otherwise noted.

All of the plastic goofies came in several different solid, multicolored, and pearlized colors, in addition to the metalized plastic (a layer of metal coating over the plastic). These goofies were sold on cards in the store using two methods. Cards consisting of all the same design or all different designs with the same theme making a set.

Therefore when you see the word *Set* it means just that. And the word *Each* means they were either sold as singles or the buttons pictured came from unrelated or incomplete sets.

Thanks to the early collectors and the Moderns Committee of the National Button Society who researched and documented these sets during the 1940s – 1960s, we can enjoy these buttons even more today!

NOTE: The following prices are what you would expect to pay if you purchased a complete set. You may pay a little less if you were to purchase them one at a time, although this process can be difficult and time consuming.

May not be shown at actual size.

Eastern Hemisphere set. Plastic, self shank, also issued as the Good Neighbors Set. $15.00 set.

Heads set. Plastic, metal shank. $15.00 set.

Ice skater, Sonja Henie, Bakelite. $6.00.

This Harper's Bazaar magazine cover is from a set of six covers. Decal on brass with metal shank. The other covers to this set are McCall's, Vogue, Red Book, Colliers, and Time. A hard set to complete. This single button is valued at $10.00.

Toy set, plastic, self shank. $15.00 set.

Dog set. Plastic, self shank. $15.00 set. This was also sold as a set of three dogs (bulldog, Scottie, and spaniel).

Celluloid Hat and Owl. Hat. $4.00. Owl. $6.00.

Sports set, another conventional set, sold in plastic and metalized plastic. $10.00 set.

Lock and Key set, metalized plastic, self shank. $5.00 set.

Cocktail set, plastic, self shank. $10.00 set.

Ace Cards set, glass, self shank. $10.00 set.

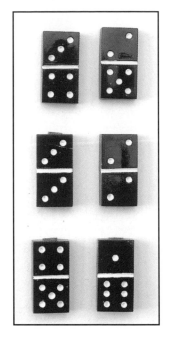

Dominoes set, plastic, self shank. $12.00 set.

Schoolroom set, plastic, self shank, conventional set. $30.00. (Shown slightly smaller than actual size.)

Mah Jongg set, plastic, self shank. $15.00 set.

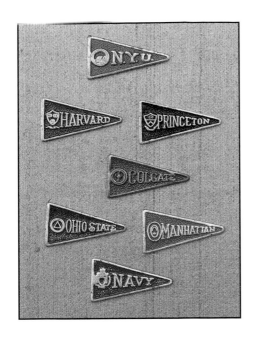

Vanity, metal with painted detail. This is one of the oldest sets. Shown three of six, missing are scissors/comb, compact/lipstick, and mirror, ca. 1930. $4.00 each.

Pennant set, metal. $22.00 set.

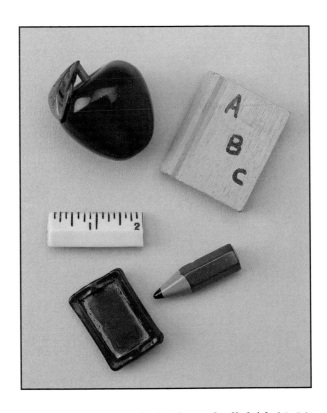

Off to school! Wood, plastic, and celluloid. $3.00 each.

Jelly Belly set, metal with glass center, sold in both gold and silver colored metal from the B. Blumenthal Company. The body stones came in several different colors, and sets with rhinestone eyes were also available. $20.00 set.

Birds on a Limb, plastic self shank, nice paint trim.
Reissues had no paint trim. $15.00 set.

Life Under the Sea set,
glass, self shank.
$18.00 set.

Hunting scenes, plastic, self shank.
This is not a realistic set because of its round
shape. It is a conventional set. $15.00 set.

License Plate set, New York World's Fair 1940.
These came in copper, gold, and silver colored
metal. $25.00 set.

*World's Fair Set, New York, 1939.
Plastic, self shank. $40.00 set.*

*Transportation set, plastic, self shank.
This set was also sold during the time
of the celebration of the 1939 World's
Fair. $18.00 set.*

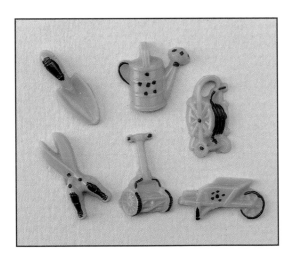

*Garden set, plastic, self shank.
$18.00 set.*

*Wedding set, plastic, self shank.
$18.00 set.*

"Arabian Pixies" *"American Pixies"*

Metal with metal shank and rhinestone trim, early 1940s, from the B. Blumenthal Company. Sets were available in gold, silver, and antiqued metal. The same set was also sold with a pearl in place of the rhinestone. $15.00 set. $15.00 set.

Yes/No set, metal, conventional set. $5.00.

Winner's Circle set, enamel on brass, conventional set. $30.00 set.

Ladies' Travel set, plastic, self shank. The belt pictured is hard to find because this set was also sold as a five piece set (not including the belt). $20.00 set.

Teenager set, plastic, self shank. $18.00 set.

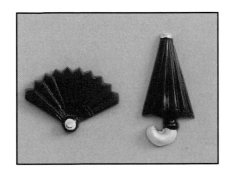

Fair and Foul Weather set, plastic, self shank. $6.00 set.

Colonel Couple, plastic, self shank. $6.00 set.

Dutch set, plastic, two-hole, paint trim. $12.00 set.

Autumn Leaves set, plastic, self shank. $10.00 set.

Folk Dancers set, plastic, self shank. $15.00 set.

Bakelite realistics. $5.00 each.

Nursery Rhyme set, Bakelite, Jack and the Beanstalk, Mother Hubbard,
Tom, Tom the Piper's Son, Old Women in the Shoe,
Little Red Riding Hood, Humpty Dumpty. $40.00.
(Shown slightly larger than actual size.)

*Circus set, plastic, self shank.
$15.00.
Note: This set is one of two
that is recognized by NBS as
realistic, not conventional.
(Shown slightly smaller
than actual size.)*

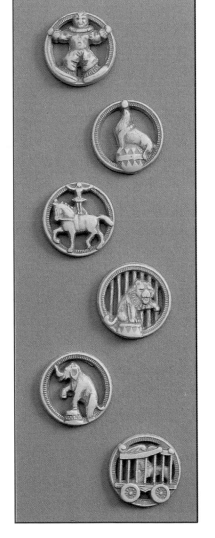

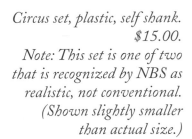

*Wooden Bowl Fruit set,
celluloid fruits in wooden bowls,
metal shank. $20.00 set.*

*Canasta set, plastic, self shank, con-
ventional set. $6.00 set.*

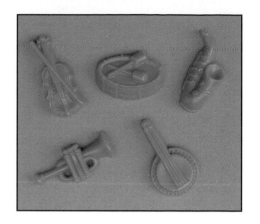

Music set, plastic, self shank.
$12.00 set.

Vase set, plastic, self shank. $12.00 set.

Circus set, plastic, self shank.
$8.00 set.

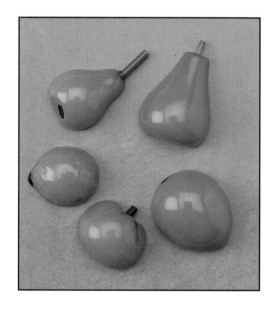

Fruit, Bakelite, metal shank,
complete set (?). $8.00 each.

Typewriter Keys set, plastic, self shank.
This is a later set from the mid 1950s.
$8.00 set.

Vegetable set, glass, self shank. This was also sold as a six-piece set not including the tomato and pepper. Therefore those two are more elusive. $20.00 set.

Good Luck Charm set, plastic, self shank. $18.00 set.

Allied Nations set, celluloid with applied celluloid shank, Great Britain, United States, and France. $10.00.

Plastic record and a Bakelite bingo card. The last button is one from a set of six called Movie Stars. Paper picture inside a metal frame with a plastic cover. They were also available in oval frames. The stars names include Errol Flynn, Tyrone Power, Robert Taylor, Myrna Loy, Loretta Young, and Clark Gable. Record. $4.00. Bingo Card. $6.00. Movie Star Picture. $8.00.

Plastic, self shank. $1.00 – $1.50.

*Mr. and Mrs. Donald Duck. $8.00 pair.
Humpty Dumpty. $4.00.
Peter Rabbit and rabbit with
basket, plastic, self shanks. $3.00 each.
Gingerbread Girl and Boy. $4.00 set.*

*Spool of thread, curler, and scissors,
celluloid and plastic. $2.00 – 4.00 each.*

*Halloween Witch and Clown set,
Bakelite. $25.00 set.
Jack-O-Lantern, Bakelite,
notice the scary mouth. $8.00.*

*Hats, metalized plastic, celluloid,
plastic, Bakelite on bottom.
$1.50 – 3.00 each.*

*Santa Claus, plastic, round plastic
shank, French goofy. $6.00.*

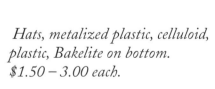

Cigarette set. This 15 pack set is from 1942, they have wooden bodies wrapped with paper labels and a metal shank. Lucky Strike cigarette buttons with white labels date to just after WWII started. Before WWII Lucky Strike labels were green. Cigarette buttons are highly collectible to both button and advertising collectors, and the ever growing numbers of tobacciana collectors. $150.00+ set.

Left: Two Bakelite packs with metal shanks. $10.00+ each.
Right: Chesterfield and Lucky Strike packs. Two from a set of five, plastic, self shanks, the decal labels are fragile and can be scratched easily. $10.00+ each.

Assorted cigarette packs. Plastic, button at bottom has metal shank, all others have plastic self shank. $7.00 – 10.00+ each.

Celluloid and plastic.
$8.00. $10.00. $6.00.

Hispanic couple. $15.00 set. French couple. $15.00 set.
College couple. $15.00 set.
Plaster like substance with brown faces and painted detail.
They have round metal rings for shanks. Notice the little
cigarette hanging from the Frenchman's mouth.

Purses, plastic and glass.
Glass. $3.00.   Plastic. $6.00.

Musical instruments. $6.00 each. Wrench, Hammer
and Screw set. $12.00. Ball and Bat set $6.00. Others.
$3.00 – 5.00.

More wood realistics. $2.00 – 5.00.

Metalized plastics.
Egyptian Head. $3.00.
Others. $1.00 – 2.00.

Mirrored two-piece glass with cemented on glass shanks.
Green glass Ladies' Toilet set, three of five, not shown
perfume bottle and mirror. $5.00 each.
Clear Animal set. $3.00 each.
Red glass Animal set, four of six. $4.00 each.

War Time buttons, 1940 – 1945, celluloid and plastic.

Armed Forces Soldier and Sailor set. Some sets coated to glow in the dark. $6.00 set.

V's, Statue of Liberty, and Thumb's Up. $2.00 – 4.00.

Al others. $1.00 – 2.00.

Celluloid, plastic, and Bakelite Key. $4.00 – 7.00.

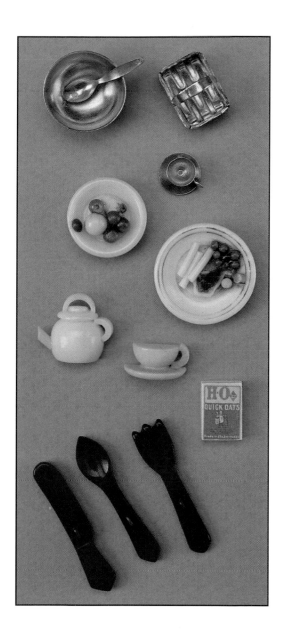

Metal mixing bowl, basket, and brass cup and saucer. $5.00 – 8.00 each.

Fruit bowl. $4.00.

Dinner plate, plastic, one of the food plates made in 1939 by the B. Blumenthal Button Co. $7.00.

Celluloid teapot and cup/saucer from a four-piece set. Tea kettle and creamer not shown. $5.00 each.

H-O Oats plastic, self shank. One from a set called Pantry Shelf, the others are Heinz Baked Beans, Domino Sugar, Lux, and Campbell Soup. $5.00 each.

Knife, spoon, and fork set, Bakelite. $20.00 set.

Card of goofies and conventionals from France. They are plastic and have round self shanks. $3.00 each.

Glass. $1.00 - $3.00.

Brass cross with glass stones. $4.00.

Fruits, celluloid, glass, and plastic. $2.00 – 4.00.

Bowling set, plastic, self shank, c. 1952.
$7.00 set.
(Shown slightly smaller than actual size.)

Ladies Sport set, plastic,
conventional, self shank.
$10.00 set.

Animal Heads set, plastic,
self-shank. $18.00 set.

Patriotic set in starred circle, plastic, self shank. $15.00 set.

Bakelite Dwarfs. $8.00+. Dwarf, glass. $10.00.
Snow White and Seven Dwarfs, plastic,
self shank, incomplete. Hard to find. $10.00 each.
Dwarf, plastic, self shank. $8.00+.

Mickey and Friends set,
plastic, self shank.
These were also sold with four of the same design on
a card marked Hollywood Button Co. $22.00 set.

Disney set, plastic, self shank.
This set was reissued with the animals
having rhinestone eyes. $8.00 set.
(Shown slightly smaller than actual size.)

More…plastic realistics. (Shown slightly smaller than actual size.)

Row 1:	$3.00	$1.50	$1.50	$1.50	$2.50	$1.50	$1.50
Row 2:	$1.50	$1.50	$1.50	$1.50	$2.00	$1.50	
Row 3:	$1.00	$1.00	$1.50	$2.00	$1.00	$1.50	
Row 4:	$1.00	$1.50	$1.50	$1.50	$1.50	$5.00	
Row 5:	$1.00	$4.00	$1.50	$1.50	$1.50	$1.00	$2.50
Row 6:	$1.50	$1.00	$1.00	$1.00	$1.00	$1.00	$1.50

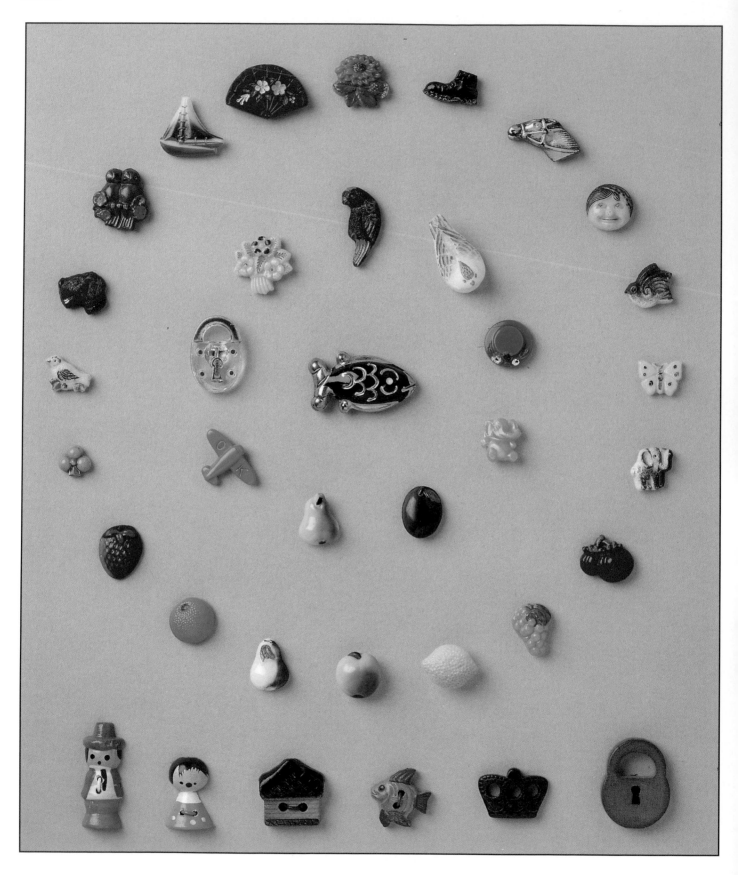

Glass. $1.00 – 2.00.   Glass Fish and Dove. $3.50.
Bottom row: Wood. $1.50 – 2.50.
(Shown slightly smaller than actual size.)

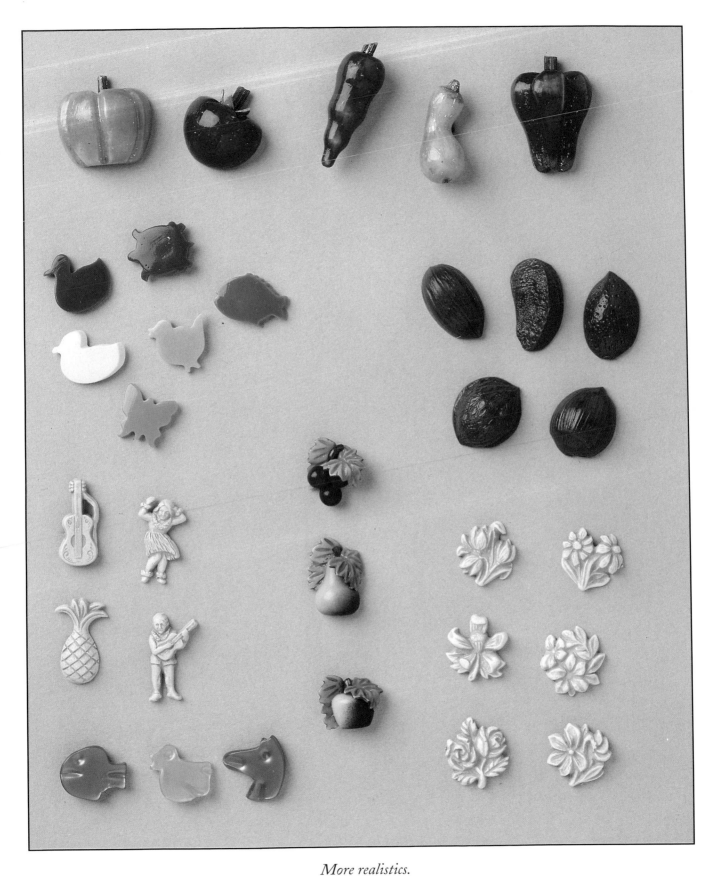

More realistics.
Vegetable set, celluloid. $15.00.   Animal set, plastic. $9.00.
Nuts, plastic, early set, later set included the peanut. $9.00.
Hawaiian set, plastic, missing the surfer. If complete $12.00.
Fruit and Double Leaves, celluloid, missing grapes, peach, and orange. If complete $12.00.
Flower set, plastic. $10.00.   Animals, plastic with celluloid shank, 1950s. $6.00

These are not realistics, but have been placed here for convenience.
More conventionals.
Row 1: Hobbies set, metal frames with paper pictures and plastic covers. $15.00 set.
Row 2: America's Map set, metalized plastic $6.00 set. Numbers set, plastic, mid–1950s. $13.00 set.
Row 3: Zodiac set, glass with applied glass shank. $15.00 set. Animal Heads set, plastic. $5.00 set
Row 4: Animal Heads set, plastic. $7.00 set. Game Words set, plastic, 1950s. $14.00.

Original cards. $8.00 – 15.00 per card.
Remember you can expect to pay less if you purchase singularly,
than if you purchase complete sets or sets on original cards!
(Shown smaller than actual size.)

Composition flecks.
Turtle and Fly. $6.00 each.
Others. $2.00.

What hard rubber buttons lack in aesthetics their variety makes up for. Collectors specialize in finding pictorials, odd colors and shapes, and rare backmarks (1849 – 1851). The 1851 date is not the date the button was manufactured, but the date Goodyear patented his more refined process of making hard rubber. Also, diminutive hard rubber buttons are not backmarked. $3.00 – 5.00 each.

Some of the company backmarks you will find are:

N.R. Co. Goodyears P=T 1851 (Novelty Rubber Co.), I.R.C. Co. Goodyear 1851 (India Rubber Comb Co.), D.H.R. Co. 1875 (Dickinson Hard Rubber Co.), A.H.R. Co. HP (American Hard Rubber Co.).

The body of these inlays are made of horn, composition, and papier-maché. In the production process for the horn and composition buttons while still pliable, white metal, pearl, and brass designs were pressed into the surface. For the papier-maché button (bottom left) the pearl chips were glued to the face and several coats of varnish were applied and polished down smooth. $3.00 – 8.00 (deer).

Assorted inlay and veneer buttons from the mid to late 1800s. Most are $2.00 – 4.00.
Top row third button. $6.00. Second row last button. $10.00. Center button, medium size. $18.00.

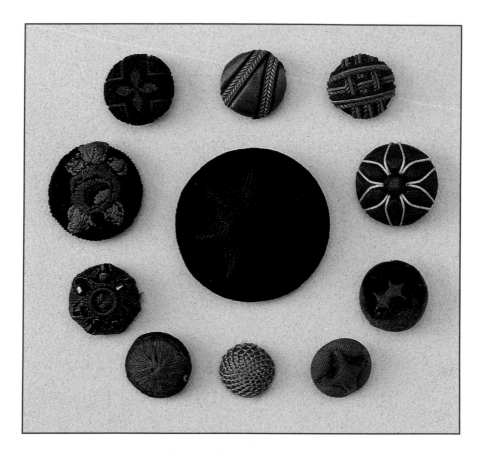

Fabric buttons cover a wide range of techniques from crocheted, embroidered, and machine woven to hand done needle work. Trims include silk thread, beads, and velvet to name a few. These representations are from 1870 – 1910 with thread backs and pad shanks. $3.00 – 7.00.

Vegetable ivory is the meat of a nut called tagua or corozo from a palm that is native to South America. Although it was used for buttons in the 1850s, it was the period of the 1870s to 1920s that production was at its highest. With the advent of the plastics industry in the 1930s and 1940s its decline was inevitable.

Vegetable ivory buttons are very common, therefore collectors are looking for more unusual examples such as large sizes, pictorials, transfer printed, and ones that are combined with other materials.

Back of a vegetable ivory button.

Red Cross. $3.00. Girl Scouts. $3.00. Lady Bug. $3.00. High Wheeler. $8.00. Collegian. $4.00.

Four-leaf clover. $4.00. Dog face. $18.00. Metal trim. $3.00.

Natural and dyed horn buttons. $4.00 – 7.00.

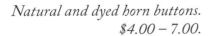

Syroco and Burwood are tradenames for buttons that
were made in Syracuse, New York, and Traverse City,
Michigan. Made of a ground wood composition,
molded and painted in several colors with brown
being the predominant, ca. 1918 – 1930s.
Boat. $3.00. Squirrel. $10.00.

Wood, all have metal shanks, the top two are
modern, the bottom is old (before 1918).
Horse head. $10.00. Bird. $8.00.
Floral urn. $15.00.

Assorted wooden buttons. $4.00 – 6.00.
(Shown smaller than actual size.)

Bone, children's underwear buttons,
these are very nice examples. $5.00 – 7.00 each.

Bone, painted underwear
button. $8.00.

Carved bone. $20.00.

Coconut shell realistics were products of the tourist trade, from
areas like the Philippine Islands during the 1930s – 1960s.
$5.00 – 8.00.

Various old and modern pictorials.

Row 1:	$8.00	$9.00	$8.00
Row 2:	$8.00	$16.00	$10.00
Row 3:	$6.00	$4.00	$5.00
Row 4:	$15.00	$7.00	$6.00

Assorted materials and subjects,
a mix of old and modern.

Row 1:	$16.00	$4.00	$5.00	$4.00
Row 2:	$5.00	$18.00	$4.00	$4.00
Row 3:	$7.00	$6.00	$1.50	$12.00
Row 4:	$3.00	$3.00	$3.50	$3.50	$6.00

(Shown slightly larger than actual size.)

 The materials and techniques used in diminutives are just as varied as their larger counterparts. The diminutives which are made of glass with painted detail are very common and can be found in every jar and tin of buttons. Collectors are looking for examples of diminutives where the material or construction of the button is harder to find in this particular size, ⅜" or smaller.

Row 1: Silvered brass with chased design. .75¢
L–R Shell. .25 - .35¢.
   Braided thread bound together with fine wire. $1.50.
   Crocheted in cream and blue. .50¢
   Green glass flower with orange glass tipped in center, loop shank plate. $1.50.
   Purple/white swirl glass with goldstone and blown glass shank. $1.50.
   Gray glass with an applied molded white glass top. $2.00.
   Stamped brass anchor with brass self-shank back. $1.50.

Row 2: Oval cobalt blue glass with incised painted design. $1.00.
L –R Design under glass. $1.00.
   Clear glass with a yellow circle overlay on purple foil set in brass, called a peacock eye. $6.00.
   Molded blue glass Jenny Lind bust set in brass. $4.00.
   Pink glass with claw set rhinestone pinhead shank and plate. $1.50.
   Black glass which was molded and painted to look like fabric called imitation fabric. .75¢.

(Shown slightly larger than actual size.)

Row 1
L–R *Twisted glass threads wrapped around a clear glass body, this type of construction is called overlay sheath. $7.00.*

Ivoroid, a term used for this type of celluloid set in metal. $5.00.

Dyed horn and inlayed with a white metal flower. $7.00.

Hard rubber with a rose design. Rubber diminutives were not backmarked like the larger sizes. $5.00.

Painted enamel on gilt brass. $4.00.

One-piece stamped and gilded brass, picturing Minerva. $5.00

China calico. $5.00.

Row 2
L–R *Moonglow. $5.00.*

Rhinestone and blue glass claw-set in brass. $4.00.

Tiny glass pieces inlayed in black glass and ground smooth, set in brass called mosaics. $27.00.

Tintype with brass rim, steel back, and wire shank. $25.00.

Peacock-eye paperweight. $6.00.

This is a Czechoslovakian paperweight button. White base with green leaves and goldstone with clear cap, loop shank, and plate. $5.00.

Lithograph with thin celluloid covering, brass rim, and steel back self-shank. $8.00.

(Shown slightly larger than actual size.)

Row 1: *Examples of common diminutives found in every old button collection. Their value has not increased as much as the harder to find diminutives. .25¢, each one with painted rose .50¢.*

Row 2: *Metal diminutives with glass centers. .75¢ – $1.00.*

Row 3: *Blue glass rose. $1.50. Blown glass ball. $2.00. Ruby glass. $1.50. Brown swirlback with white overlay. $1.50. Blue glass with paint filled lines. $1.00. Green glass with stone. $1.50.*

Row 4: *One-piece brass with floral design. $1.50. Blue mirror attached to a wide plate with loop shank. $2.00. Rhinestone, claw set. $2.00. Brass with celluloid background. $1.50. Composition fleck ball. $1.00. Blue glass center with riveted steel border. $1.50.*

Studio buttons are buttons made specifically for collectors and as a general rule were not used on clothing or sold commercially!

Renae Kitchen of Button Impressions in Colorado Springs, Colorado, made this ceramic (white clay) button. This is a replica of an old button. She has been making buttons since 1992. It is backmarked "Renae 93" attached plastic shank. $3.00.

Indian pot by Lynne Mead of Michigan. She has been making femo clay and decoupage buttons since 1990 and backmarks her work with "Lynne" or "Wooden Button Studio," ca. 1992. $4.00.

Julie Clinton of Blue Flame Studios in Bellingham, WA, made these lampworked glass buttons. She is also known for her glass beads and has taught and exhibited extensively on the subject. She has been making buttons since 1991, ca. 1995. $40.00.

Photo courtesy of Julie Clinton.

Caption for photo on page 148:
All of these clay buttons are backmarked $\frac{E}{T}$ (E over T). The majority are of red clay with just a couple in white clay. I purchased these on two separate occasions from old button collections from Battle Creek, Michigan. There is an ad in the back of the March 1964 National Button Society bulletin where a dealer was selling some of these she had purchased from the Nora Wilson estate button collection, proving that they were made before 1964. Another interesting fact is that Nora B. Wilson is listed as a member of the National Button Society as of July 1949 with an address of Battle Creek, Michigan. Now this does not yet prove who made them but it is my personal opinion that they were made in Michigan. Through talking to family members I found out that two of the three collectors were not members of national or local clubs and didn't even own one book on buttons. One collector was a member of National from 1949 to 1955, so it seems very unlikely to me that she would have known about or purchased these from out of state. I have been given one name but until I do further research the mystery of who ET is continues! $3.00 – 10.00 each.

See page 147 for information.

This large porcelain button with a transfer printed rose and gold painted spiderweb was made by Edith Morlock. It has a large saucer-shaped shank with holes on each side, backmarked "Edith 1964." $6.00.

Both of these ceramic buttons were made by Helen Babbington. White ceramic with self shank. They have her name scratched in the back, ca. 1940s. $6.00 each.

During the 1960s – early 1970s Benjamin Lang of Michigan made buttons in which he encased drawings and paper cut-outs in acrylic. The button to the left is unusual because here he used enameled metal findings. The flat metal shank is heavily glued in. Both backmarked "Ben L 67." $12.00. $5.00.

Two examples of Shirley Shaw's Jasperware buttons. Both are backmarked "Shirley 89." She has been making buttons since 1972. $4.00 each.

*Calvary. backmarked "*D. Evans & Co.* Attleboro Mass." $15.00.*
Indiana State Seal, backmarked with 10 stars and a circle around the shank. $3.00.
New Mexico State Seal, backmarked "Waterbury Button Co." $4.00.
*Massachusetts State Seal, backmarked "*****Treble*****Gilt." $6.00.*
Kentucky State Seal, backmarked. "Pettibone Mf'g Co. Cincinnati." $4.00.

Queen Elizabeth II, cast metal with bronze-colored finish. Made for her coronation celebration in 1953. $25.00 set.

Vermont Militia. $40.00.
Artillery 1808 – 1821. $45.00.
Phoenix No. 8. $15.00+.
Harrison and Reform. $45.00.
Western Union Telegraph. $4.00.
Louisiana Purchase Expo. $10.00.
Post Office Dept. $5.00.

Trylon and Perisphere, 1939 New York World's Fair. Two-piece brass, backmarked "Waterbury Button Co." $5.00.

On a hunting trip in 1902, President Roosevelt's refusal to kill a young bear cub caught the public's attention. Soon, manufacturers were marketing their stuffed bears as teddy bears. This button and a few others were inspired from this event, worn on children's clothing. $8.00.

Billy Possum was the prevailing nickname for Howard Taft, Theodore Roosevelt's successor for the presidency in 1908. Also, a children's clothes button. $12.00.

This black glass button came out of a political organization called the Union League Club, founded in 1862. They were supporters of Lincoln and the Republican Party. I have seen several, but this example is in reverse. $12.00.

Tortoise shell with white metal inlay mounted in a brass rim, steel back, and wire shank. $65.00.

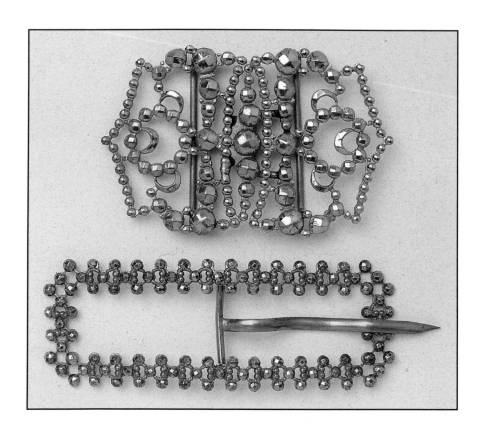

Top: Stamped and silvered brass, imitating cut steels. $15.00.
Bottom: This buckle has cut steels that have been individually
riveted to the metal framework. $12.00.

Top: Stamped brass with six marcasites and green center stone. $24.00.
Middle: Silvered brass with Art Nouveau design, backmarked ⟨C&R⟩. $35.00.
Bottom: Gold colored metal with rhinestones. $10.00.

Faceted squares of black glass with silver luster mounted in a white metal frame. $18.00.

Top: Celluloid tops with metal backs, matching button and buckle. $12.00 pair.

Bottom: Bakelite with rhinestones. $20.00.

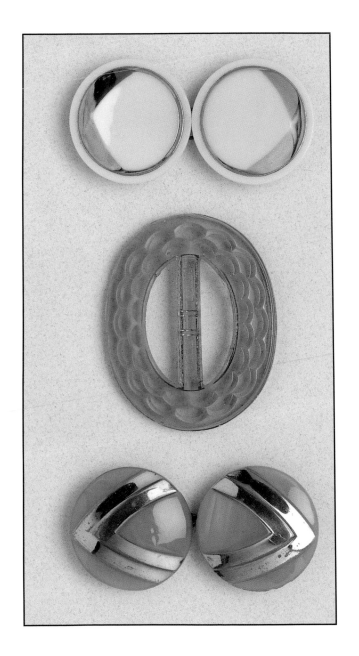

*White glass buckle with silver luster,
backmarked "Made in Czechoslovakia." $10.00.
Yellow glass, backmarked "Czech Slov." $3.00.
Glass with gold and silver luster, backmarked
"Registered Made in Czechoslovakia." $10.00.*

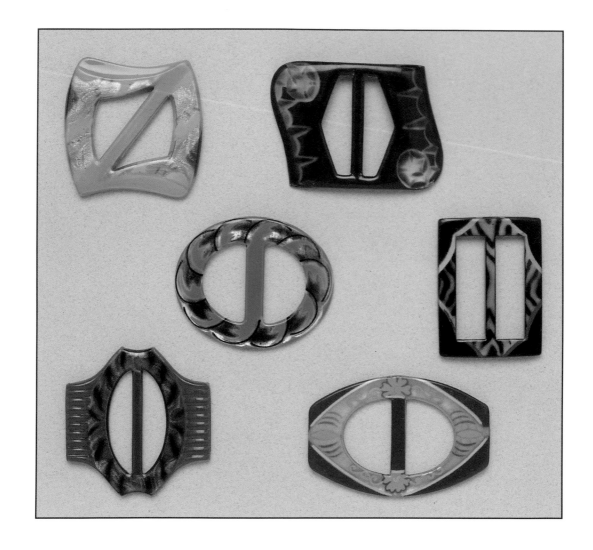

All the buckles in this grouping have a thin sheet of celluloid which extends over the edge securing the metal back. The two far left examples have foil which shines through the celluloid. One is backmarked "Czechoslovakia" all others marked "Germany." $3.00 – 5.00 each.

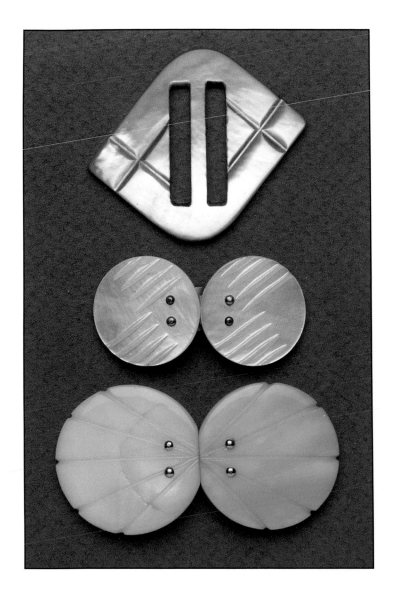

Pearl buckles, the top and bottom buckles were dyed.
Top: $2.00 – $4.00. $6.00.

Wood. $4.00.

Top: Celluloid with metal back. $18.00.
Bottom: Molded celluloid. $35.00.

*Dress elevators were used to decorate the outer
skirt of a dress by doubling up the material
to make ruffles or flounces.
Not all ends of the screw were sharp and may
have been used in another decorative purpose.
Ca. 1850s – 1880s. $3.00 – 5.00 each.*

*Snappettes.
The bottom example is unsnapped to show where the small holes
are for sewing onto your clothing. $5.00 – 10.00.*

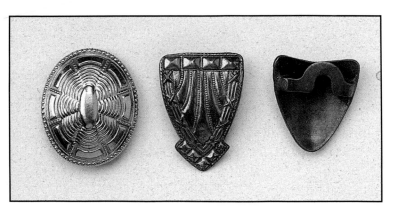

*Shoe button covers, ca. 1910 – 1920s. The shoes of this time
period had a strap that went across the top of the foot and
attached at one side with a small button. The far right
example shows the backside of the cover which slid down
over the button for decoration. $8.00 matching pair.*

*China studs. Most of these were purchased as blanks and
then handpainted or transfer printed at home. They
were popular between the late 1800s and early 1900s.
Top row: $18.00. $24.00.
Center: Back of a china stud.
Bottom row: $7.00. $7.00.*

Cape clasps.
Top: Bakelite. $25.00.
Middle: Bakelite. $25.00.
Bottom: White metal. $20.00.

Prices for photo on page 161:

Bird set. $15.00.	Regal set. $8.00.	Violin. $6.00.
Dancers set. $18.00.	Three-Little Indians. $18.00.	Guard. $7.00.
	Thanksgiving set. $18.00.	
Oriental set. $22.00.		Antique set. $22.00.
Sword set. $8.00.		Fleur-de-lis, front and back. $1.00.

Tac-back scatter pins are whimsical clothing accessories, popular from the 1940s to the 1960s.
I have also heard them called pinch backs.

See page 160 for information.

$2.00 per card.

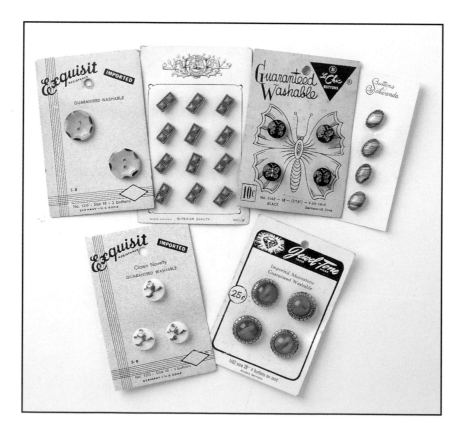

Top row: Card. $3.00 – 5.00.
Bottom row: Clowns. $7.00.   Moonglows. $10.00.

Buttons on original store cards.

The End

$8.00.
The devil made me do this book!
—DJW

The Big Book of Buttons by Elizabeth Hughes and Marion Lester, reprinted in 1991 and available from New Leaf Publishers in Augusta, Maine. A very large and thorough guide for the serious button collector.

The Collector's Encyclopedia of Buttons by Sally C. Luscomb, reprinted in 1992 by Schiffer Publishing of Pennsylvania. Aside from the fact that most of the buttons pictured in this text are black and white, you will find a lot of information on buttons that is not found in other books. A book that every collector should own.

About Buttons by Peggy Ann Osborne, 1994, also available from Schiffer Publishing. Deals heavily on time periods and how our culture was reflected on buttons.

There are many more button books that are out of print, but can be found through button dealers.

One of the best resources available for collectors right now is *The National Button Bulletin* printed five times a year at the current cost of $15.00/yr. Included in each issue are pictures of buttons, informative articles, button dealer advertisements, and button show dates. A bargain and a must for all collectors! To become a member of the National Button Society contact:

Miss Lois Pool, Secretary
2733 Juno Place
Akron, Ohio 44333-4137

Checks payable to:
National Button Society

Another valuable tool for collectors is the out of print issues of *Just Buttons* magazine printed from the early 1940s to the late 1970s. For many years collectors looked forward to every issue. Sadly missed back issues can be purchased from button dealers.

The following dealers carry both out-of-print button books and back issues of Just Buttons *magazines and* National *bulletins:*

Mary Lucas
92 Mt. Vernon Rd.
Plantsville, CT 06479

M. W. Speights
5707 Greencraig
Houston, TX 77035

For superior Swarovski stones, from crystal (clear) to colored in all sizes contact:
Stella & Paul's Unique
9205 Ridge Blvd.
Brooklyn, NY 11209
1-718-833-1566

Quality Electric Erasing Machines, information available from:
Alvin & Company, Inc.
1335 Blue Hills Ave.
Bloomfield, CT 06002
1-860-243-8991
I use Model EE175. Eraser Refills, soft green No. 75

Button Collecting Supplies:
Phil Linley
232 Linley Dr.
Fairfield, CT 06432
Mounting board, button spiders, wire, cleaning kits, and templates, also his personally designed Linley button measure, a must have.

Mack & Mary's
63 Bacon St.
Meriden, CT 06450
Specializing in drop-in wooden display frames with glass fronts, also carry mounting cards, button spiders, and more.

Button Images
1317 Lynndale Rd.
Madison, WI 53711-3316
Design cards, wire, heavy gauge vinyl display envelopes, project cards, and scanning of button photos, etc. Drop them a line and they will gladly send you their information and price list.

Local and State Societies
Most states have their own local clubs and state societies. A list is included in the National Button Society's Directory when you become a member.
My own state's bulletin is available at a cost of $7.00 per year (3 issues).
Checks payable to:
 Michigan Button Society.
 Send to:
 Ulta Loew, Treasurer
 133 E. LeGrand
 Howell, MI 48843

I also recommend the Buckeye State Button Society Bulletin, dues are $10.00 for 3 issues a year.
Checks Payable to:
 Buckeye State Button Society.
 Send to:
 Mrs. Laura Gene Chisnell
 400 E. Clinton St.
 Doylestown, OH 44230-1507

Index